HOW TO GET THE MOST OUT OF LIFE

D1598858

Books by Paul A. Hauck

The Three Faces of Love

Overcoming Jealousy and Possessiveness

Brief Counseling with RET

How to Stand Up for Yourself

Marriage Is a Loving Business

How to Do What You Want to Do: The Art of Self-Discipline

Overcoming Worry and Fear

Overcoming Frustration and Anger

Overcoming Depression

HOW TO GET
THE MOST OUT OF LIFE

Paul A. Hauck

Westminster/John Knox Press
LOUISVILLE, KENTUCKY

First published in Great Britain
in 1988 by Sheldon Press

Copyright © Paul Hauck 1988

All rights reserved — no part of this book may be reproduced
in any form without permission in writing from the publisher,
except by a reviewer who wishes to quote brief passages
in connection with a review in magazine or newspaper.

First American edition

Published by Westminster/John Knox Press
Louisville, Kentucky

Printed in the United States of America
9 8 7 6 5 4 3 2 1

Library of Congress Cataloging-in-Publication Data

Hauck, Paul A.
    How to get the most out of life / Paul A. Hauck. — 1st American
    ed.
        p.   cm.
    ISBN 0-664-25114-5
    1. Self-actualization (Psychology) 2. Rational-emotive
psychotherapy. I. Title.
BF637.S4H375 1990
158'.1—dc20

90-32094
CIP

I dedicate this book to me. After all I've written, why not? It's my turn.

It's also dedicated to my grandson Alex.

Contents

1 What Is Self-neglect?   1

2 Think for Yourself   5

3 Faulty Thinking   12

4 Control Yourself   33

5 Enough Is Enough   57

6 Friendship and Social Skills   82

7 Health and Wealth   95

8 Hold Your Head High   109

1

What Is Self-neglect?

I want you to try and imagine that your life is about to draw to a close. You are lying on your deathbed reflecting on what you've achieved. Ask yourself if you've really enjoyed life. Are you glad you were born? Have you had a good time? Are your friends and loved ones truly sorry to see you go, and will you be missed? If you could live your life all over again would you live it in exactly the same way? Can you in all honesty say to yourself: 'It's been nice. It's been exciting. I made the most of it'? If you can, you do *not* suffer what I call *self-neglect*.

Ask most people what they understand by self-neglect and they'll tell you things like not brushing your teeth twice a day, not visiting the dentist every six months, or not taking regular baths. Although these aspects of self-neglect are obviously important, in this book I will be using the term in a much wider sense. In brief, people who suffer from self-neglect feel guilty about taking the slightest interest in themselves. As a consequence of this they get depressed. They don't enjoy good health. They fail to use their money wisely. They let others trample all over them. They have few, if any, friends. They do not get the best out of life. Life, in fact, passes them by. Let's consider a few examples.

Gayle thought that the way to ensure a happy marriage was to be her husband John's devoted slave. She neglected her own wants and needs, ministering instead entirely to his — he never even had to run his own bath! She never complained out loud when he left her at home in front of the TV while he went out for the evening with his friends. She seldom spent any money on herself so that there would be more for him. Her sacrifices, she thought, could only make him love her more and more. It would get too much for her sometimes, and she would protest. But he would lose his temper, scream the

1

house down, and threaten to leave her. She would suffer bouts of anxiety or anger. The rest of the time she would get depressed. She had periodic headaches, and became obese.

Mabel wanted her children, in-laws, and other members of the family to visit her often, to spend holidays at her home. She would get annoyed if they couldn't. She also had the sorry habit of expressing herself in the bluntest possible manner and never understood why this caused offence. So if her family stayed away, she would tear into them for their standoffishness. This spiral inevitably fed on itself to the point where she was deserted by the entire family.

Tom spent his every working day at an office desk. He worked late, took work home, even worked at weekends. He took no serious exercise. He paid no attention to his diet, eating as much as he pleased of whatever he wanted, and drinking so much that he sported a gut that made him look as if he was pregnant with twins. One day, while playing touch football with his teenage sons, he had a heart attack and died.

Audrey was widowed at fifty-two. Her husband left behind a decent estate, all of which went to her. Instead of getting professional advice from a financial consultant, she invested the money as she thought best. What was left she kept no proper control over — loaning money to relatives, spending money on travel, and drawing regularly on her savings account. She went into retirement with only a fraction of the money she could have had.

All these people neglected themselves in some way or other. Gayle's problem was that she was too tolerant and passive. Mabel was self-centred and aggressive. Tom did not look after his health. Audrey was careless with money. Perhaps you can recognize yourself or other people in one or more of these four examples. Perhaps you think they are examples of normal behaviour. Well, they are in so far as there are a lot of Gayles, Mabels, Toms and Audreys among us. But you don't have to be like them if you don't want to. This book can show you how.

In this book, then, I will set out to teach you how to overcome the problem of self-neglect. You will learn the art of enlightened self-interest. You may well think I am taking on the impossible, that I have bitten off more than I can chew. Well, ask yourself this. Just what is it that marks out those who live contented lives and make the most of their talents and resources from the rest who don't? Perhaps they're endowed with some special gift which you're either lucky to have been born with or not.

Not so. They're human, too, you know! In thirty years' observing human behaviour as a clinical psychologist, I have come to the conclusion that it is within the power of anyone with average intelligence who is reasonably practical to take control of his life and to get much more out of it. The behaviours that prevent us from doing this can be reduced to only a few categories. Provided you follow a few straight-forward guidelines, you, too, can do it. There really is no need for you to continue to be your worst enemy!

First, it is important that you learn to be able to think for yourself. In Chapter 2 we look at the reasons why people fail to do this. They are trained not to think because of their upbringing or childhood training; because of their fear of rejection; because of their self-distrust; because of their laziness; or because they let others do their thinking for them. You must take courage and refuse to behave like sheep.

Second, you must learn to avoid the kind of thinking which is faulty. Those who are naïve or fanatical can be said to be prone to faulty thinking, as are those whose thinking is dominated by certain 'myths' and 'superstitions' which they go through life accepting without question. We look as these in Chapter 3. They don't in fact stand up to detailed scrutiny.

Third, you must learn to master such harmful 'neurotic' emotions as depression, anger, fear, and jealousy, and to avoid procrastination. In Chapter 4 you will learn what causes these emotional disturbances. Much of this chapter is based on the work of Dr Albert Ellis's theory of Rational Emotive

Therapy (RET). Ellis identified a number of irrational beliefs which cause us to experience certain emotional conditions. We list these and try to overturn them.

Fourth, you must learn how to stand up for yourself; to avoid excessive tolerance or passivity. How happy you are depends to a large extent on the degree of co-operation, respect and love you get from other people. Provided that you can assert yourself without giving in to certain harmful emotions, you will learn easily to get and maintain the co-operation, respect and love of those who matter to you. In Chapter 5 we show you how.

Fifth, in developing the social skills you need to get and maintain friends, you must learn to overcome shyness, and to avoid aggression and self-centredness. This is the subject of Chapter 6.

Finally, you must learn to look after your health and wealth. This is the subject of Chapter 7.

Read on, not once but several times. You cannot grasp all I have to offer from a single reading. And do not write off any of my ideas which may seem far-fetched or impractical until you've tried them. I speak from experience, not speculation. Imagine yourself on your deathbed again. Wouldn't you like to look over your life and pronounce it a 'job well done'?

2

Think for Yourself

We all have different strategies for coping with the problems life presents us, but however we choose to go about this, we all have at our disposal the use of an organ which is capable of solving problems of the utmost complexity — our brain. How stange, then, that so many of us simply fail to put it to good use!

Now I'm not saying that each and every one of us is always capable of coming to a decision about something without help from anybody else. If you don't have enough information to help you make a decision, then seek advice from someone who knows more than you do. But there will come a point when, once you've got all the facts you need, the decision will have to be made, and you will be on your own. To make the decision which is best for you, you have to be able to think for yourself.

How to be a non-thinker

Many of you reading this book are not thinkers: you either cannot or will not think for yourselves. This is an aspect of your self-neglect which you can readily overcome if you apply yourself to it. In doing so, it is critical that you understand how people become non-thinkers. It has been my experience that people are raised to become non-thinkers in five different ways.

Childhood training

The way we are raised determines to a large degree how we use our thinking skills. Some children have it drummed into them that they must obey unquestioningly. They must believe what they are told. They are encouraged not to think, not to ask questions, not to turn a thought over in their minds and to arrive at conclusions on their own. Some parents and teachers are rigid individuals who are afraid to be challenged and who, for their own convenience, want obedience from children rather than curiosity. They are usually very insecure people who cannot stand being questioned. For them children are good only when they obey and respect their elders. It never occurs to them that children who ask interesting and challenging questions are a delight to their parents, are fun to rear, wonderful to talk with, and go on to become stimulating adults.

Sometimes parents are afraid to be outshone. Perhaps they have no authority in any other area of their lives so they make sure that their home is their castle and their children are their subjects. In fact, for their children to aspire higher than their parents is thought to be an insult. One of my clients told me that he desired to rise higher than his father but was repeatedly squelched by both his parents. His mother shockingly stated on more than one occasion: 'Don't you think for one minute that you are any better than your father. Working in a factory was good enough for him and it's good enough for you. So don't get any high and mighty airs. Know your place in the world.'

Could more discouraging words ever be uttered to a child? How can a youngster dare to think for himself after being told such a thing? No progress can come from such a rearing, for love is given only if the child remains ignorant and obedient. Disapproval is always meted out when the child's natural curiosity and intelligence seeks to understand the whys and wherefores of this world. Such an upbringing is equivalent to drugging the child's brain so that it cannot be exercised. The brain becomes a relatively useless organ when it is not allowed to speculate, fantasize, daydream, and, most of all, disagree.

Fear of rejection

The two greatest fears we humans possess seem to be the fear of rejection and the fear of failure. In many cases the fear of doing badly is actually an outcome of the fear of rejection. If one does poorly then one is sometimes rejected. It is for this reason that I view the fear of rejection as one of the greatest of all the common fears, and the fear of mistakes and failures as the second most frequent and serious fear.

Try to imagine for a moment how few people are going to raise challenging and differing views if they are going to experience feelings of inferiority because their views might be incorrect. And likewise, how little thinking will be done if a person fears that rejection by important persons will be the result.

How pathetic it is that we are so afraid of rejection. We act throughout our lives as though we must always have the approval and love of those who are important to us. As children this is, of course, not an unreasonable concern. But one sees this equally strongly among young *and* mature adults. What is usually the outcome of disagreeing with those we are close to? Are we always rejected? Are we always fired from a job? Are we always expelled from school? Hardly. As a matter of fact, common observation has it that those people who think the most originally are usually the most respected. They are instantly seen as bright people who have leadership qualities and who can add something to a situation rather than simply reflect the prevailing attitudes.

It is critical, in order to be a true thinker, to take the slight risk of being rejected, since this *in itself* is not painful. To be rejected is sometimes inconvenient and may cost us a relationship, but that is hardly as serious as it is to have a relationship at the cost of becoming a dunce. Rejection is not painful *unless you make it so*. Once you get it into your head that you do not need a particular person's love and respect, you will change the forces that stifle your very growth. Those who would have you agree with everything they wish are not your friends. They are holding you back. A true and caring person encourages your growth by giving you the freedom to think and perhaps disagree. Foolish though your thoughts

7

may be, on whatever subject, you are still better off expressing them so that they can be brought into the open, analysed, debated, and then, perhaps, rejected. If you are forced to keep them to yourself, you haven't the slightest chance of learning anything.

To think daringly and imaginatively usually means to think differently. Thinking differently is something threatening to those insecure people around us who do not like change or who do not like to be challenged over their pet beliefs. The person who says 'How dare you think that way? What makes you so right all the time? Who do you think you are, God?' is committing a grievous fault against another human being's growth. If we disagree with other people's utterances, so be it. Let us disagree. And let us discuss and debate and challenge people's beliefs. But let us never, for heaven's sake, never tell them that they cannot have their thoughts. When we do insist on this we are committing a bigger fault than the person we are disagreeing with.

Self-distrust

A sense of inferiority is practically always present in those who have never been cautioned to think for themselves. When we have a germ of self-doubt and we distrust ourselves, it becomes extremely difficult for us to think in daring and exciting ways. We will usually wonder 'Who am I to think that I am right and everyone else is wrong? I'm nothing, I'm uneducated, so how can I be so sure I am right?'

If you let your feelings of inferiority scare you from thinking freely, then again you will be stymied and silenced even though you may have the most productive mind in the world. Let's face it, some of the more brilliant thoughts have appeared to us at first glance throughout history to be absurd and stupid. For example, in the days when the world was believed to be flat, anyone who dared to say it was round was at best laughed at, at worst persecuted. That all people are equal, that one race is as potentially capable as another, that women are the equals of men, each of these notions has had to conquer disbelief and ridicule. The idea that man could go to the moon was also dismissed with contempt.

The history of man's progress is filled with examples of beliefs which were thought ridiculous at one time and later became fully accepted. Today's nonsense may well be tomorrow's truth. Practically every great idea has to fight through a shell of ignorance and resistance in order to achieve birth. But the struggle will not take place in those individuals who feel they must be wrong because they feel inferior to others, and must defer to those who are wealthy, powerful, or educated. There may well be some measure of truth in the notion that the wealthy, the educated, or the powerful achieved that status because they were better informed. That hardly means, however, that everything they have to say is blessed with truth and everything anyone else says is not. Being rich, powerful or educated is by no means a guarantee that the beliefs of these people are correct a vast majority of the time and the beliefs of those less fortunate are always incorrect.

An inferiority complex is the most serious of psychological conditions which can be imposed upon anyone if the brainwashing takes place early enough and is done vigorously enough. A genius can come to believe that he is inferior if his faults are pointed out endlessly and he is given no credit or encouragement for his achievements. Once we get over the idea that mistakes make us worthless we can then begin to develop a sense of pride in ourselves and realize that our efforts, however inadequate, are healthy measures for achieving knowledge. We are not inferior as people if we happen to be inferior in some particular respect. Mistakes are not terrible, they do not indicate failure, and they certainly do not indicate that we are inferior. They are extremely important stepping stones to further knowledge and higher levels of success. A mistake is not something carved in marble forever. If you are wrong on one occasion that doesn't mean you can never be right again!

Laziness

To think requires energy. It is exercise for the brain just as running is exercise for the body. Overweight people, because they shun the exercise necessary to keep themselves physically trim, accumulate weight and get less exercise because it becomes more and more strenuous. It seems to me the same happens with the brain. If you are a lazy thinker, then it is going to become easier for you *not* to think. The less you think the less you want to think.

Perhaps you know someone who has taken up running and become physically fit. Well you can do to your brain what that person has done to his body. And you don't have to venture out of doors on cold and frosty mornings to do it! If someone tells you something and you have a suspicion that it isn't true then force yourself to think about it until you are convinced it either is or isn't true. The more you do that the easier it gets— the more you run the further and faster you can run. And don't say you can't think. The fact that you had a suspicion that what you were told wasn't true means that you started a thought, even if you didn't take it very far. Think about it!

Received ideas

It is all too easy not to think for yourself and let others, those in authority perhaps, experts, those who 'ought to know what they're talking about', do your thinking for you. You take for granted that the beliefs held by respected authorities and society at large are correct and should not be questioned. You live your life the way others tell you to. You feel guilty if prompted to do anything differently. But stop and consider the consequences of this for a moment. If nothing were open to question, if nobody ever thought an original thought, nothing would ever be discovered or invented and society would simply stand still. But society does not stand still.

People do challenge the received ideas of the day, and thus society progresses.

Other people go against the trend, think original thoughts. Nobody can stop you doing the same if you want to. To think for yourself, to start from the position that any statement or belief may, or may not, be true, whatever other people say, and to examine it for yourself, is an act of courage. Be daring in this enterprise. No matter how sacred the idea, dare to choose whether to accept it or not. You are free to think as you choose.

Conclusion

It is about time we realized that most of us are sheep. We are followers and will believe anyone who seems impressive enough. We do not think, we simply obey. To go against the common herd is apparently an extremely difficult thing for human beings to do. You cannot be a creative person, nor probably a very interesting one, unless you are willing to think for yourself. Only when you are not afraid of being criticized do you release your creative powers to think along original lines.

A study carried out at the University of California examined the temperaments of people who scored high on creative intelligence. It was found that they had a number of characteristics in common: sensitivity, impulsiveness, lack of inhibition, a desire to be active, and a lack of respect for things conventional. The greatest courage a person can show is to advance an idea that seems right and to resist one that seems wrong. The gift of independent human thought can conquer a great many of our defects. If you must be afraid of something, be afraid of *not* thinking.

3

Faulty Thinking

An important step in taking a healthy interest in yourself, in overcoming self-neglect, is to learn to become smart about life. Being smart about life is about not being gullible or naïve. It is about being practical, knowing how to get to the heart of the matter without being side-tracked, how to cut through the fat of an issue so as to see it for what it really is. Certainly, you have to think for yourself. But you must also avoid faulty thinking. In studying the ways people fail to do themselves justice, I have found that the faulty thinking which is often responsible falls into three distinct categories: myths and superstitions; fanaticism; and naïvety. We will take a look at each of these in turn.

Myths and Superstitions

When I speak of myths and superstitions I am not talking about the usual superstitions we are all exposed to as children. I am not referring to the bad luck which supposedly comes when a black cat crosses your path, or to the untold horrors you'll suffer if you break a mirror. Whether you toss salt over your left shoulder if you spill some is, for my present purposes, neither here nor there. I'm not going to ask you to question the existence of spooks and ghosts. I am going to assume that you have given up these childish beliefs and put them wherever you put your beliefs about Father Christmas.

The kinds of myths and superstitions I'm referring to are those which many people believe and live by, often to their detriment, throughout their entire lives. Some of them even have a grain of truth to them, but they will never fail to hold you back if you place too much faith in them. It may never have occurred to you to question them, so you may not realize how much harm believing them can cause you. Let me give you some examples.

'You can do anything and be anything you want.' It is, of course, perfectly true that the human species has been and is able to do an incredible number of quite amazing things. The miracles of science, the wonders of architecture, the glory of music and art, are all the product of man's genius. When he landed on the moon he was only continuing in that same tradition of doing what appeared to be impossible.

That said, however, it is possible to take this idea too far, as some parents do when they urge their children on to heights and dreams which are simply beyond them. The young college science student who appeared before me dejected, depressed, and feeling inadequate lived by that idea that anything was possible if he tried hard enough. He was told to study and earn the grades that would get him into post-graduate studies and then into a profession that would give him a comfortable life. However, he was not suited to go into the sciences. He wanted to work in the arts. No matter how hard he tried he simply could not manage physics, calculus and organic chemistry — not because he wasn't bright enough, he simply didn't have the kind of mind-set which handled that kind of material. He did not realize that there are different types of intelligence: some of us can write or paint but cannot dance; others are gifted in athletics but not in mathematics. And no matter how hard some of us try, and despite the well-intentioned urgings of our parents and teachers, we will never never reach the goals that are sometimes set for us by people who continually insist that we can do anything we want if we put our hearts and souls into it.

So be gentle with yourself. Do not neglect yourself by hating both your inadequacies *and* yourself when you aren't able to do something beyond your natural gifts. You abuse yourself if you do. The least of the consequences you will feel are a sense of failure, guilt and depression for having failed and disappointed those who felt you could do anything merely because you seem to show some talent in other ways.

'Money is the root of all evil.' As with other superstitions I will address, this also has a germ of truth in it. The pursuit of money and wealth has indeed driven people to desperate measures: murder, torture, deception, and other base human behaviours have been directly linked to the overwhelming drive to gain wealth.

However, if you take this myth literally, as some people do, you will deny yourself some of the greatest pleasures, securities, and comforts that are possible on this earth. If money is such a filthy thing to have then why is it that the poorest people in the world are among the most miserable? Ask the people in the slums whether they would not trade places with the people in the suburbs. Ask those who own old bangers and are forever spending their hard-earned dollars on repairing them if they wouldn't give their eye teeth for a new car.

'The best things in life are free' is a superstition which is closely related to this one. It is as though someone were trying to convince us that we should not work hard and not strive for material possessions. The best things in life cost the earth. Clean water does not come free. Clean air is extremely costly. Food is not free, nor are clothing, housing, and practically anything else that makes life comfortable. It may well be different in the South Seas where you can sunbathe on the sand and reach up and pick a banana. Money is not essential in such an environment. However, practically anywhere else where there is any semblance of a civilized society, money is the root of a great deal of good.

The love of money, if it is done to excess and if it is so all-consuming that it is loved for its own sake rather than for the good it can do for oneself and others, is indeed an evil. Unfortunately, people who are naïve and neglect themselves trouble themselves greatly over acquiring comfort and feel very guilty over the fruits of their labours. One young lady, who had always been poor, went into selling insurance and began to make commissions she had never dreamed of. She consulted me over the guilt this new-found wealth gave her. She seriously thought of quitting her job because she didn't think she could have it so good because she had always been taught that money is bad. How sad!

'Everything happens for the best.' If this is so then tell me what is so wonderful about an earthquake wiping out an Italian village on a mountainside? What is so wonderful about a member of your family drowning? What is so wonderful about being injured, or living in poverty, or being kidnapped or killed?

All these situations are rotten to the core. They bring immense suffering to the victims. If you still believe there is great merit in those things then we simply don't agree. I would certainly go along with you if you said that we should try to make the best out of any bad situation. But that is hardly the same as saying that all the bad things that happen to us are in fact good things.

'What will be will be.' This sounds like a statement you can hardly question. It seems self-evident. How, for example, could anything which will be, not be? It expresses the inevitability of some events, such as growing old, or that one season will follow another, or that there will probably always be wars among men. We take it for granted that certain things will be and that there is nothing we can do about some of them.

I want to call this piece of 'wisdom' into question by looking at it from another point of view. People whose thinking is faulty can harm themselves erroneously believing that certain events are inevitable and then, having accepted that fate, predicting an event and then making it happen: the self-fulfilling prophecy. Let me give you an example. During the Second World War I frequently heard soldiers comment that they didn't have to worry about a mortar shell or bullet hitting them unless it had their 'number' on it.

Notice how absurd this whole notion is. If you stick your head above ground and manage not to get hit, you're correct to say that you were lucky. But, to say that you weren't hit because none of the bullets had your number on it simply doesn't make sense. They all missed you and you are still alive. Any or all of the bullets could have had your number on them if the enemy had been a better shot. You didn't get hit because you were lucky.

Similarly, some people take a fatalistic attitude towards behaviours which involve risk or chance — for example, gambling — or simple everyday decisions as to which school to send their children to, or whether to take a particular trip. These same people will get on an aeroplane and then reason that there is no point in worrying about having an accident unless it was meant for them to have an accident. Do you see how they believe that their fates are controlled by some invisible force? Instead of appreciating the fact that it is up to them to *make* events happen as they want them to, they surrender control over their lives.

My advice is to follow the wisdom of Shakespeare when he suggests that our fate is not in our stars but in ourselves.

'Justice is blind.' If justice is truly blind then it must follow that the innocent will always be freed and the guilty will always be punished. Power and influence will have no effect on the outcome of a verdict, nor will a man's colour or his religion. If justice is blind then the legal system must work perfectly at all times, and lawyers who are on the 'wrong' side of the issue must always lose. Judges must always be Solomons and never have a bad day, never get out of bed on the wrong side, and never have family problems which distract them from their heavy duties while in the courtroom.

Obviously this is nothing more than a flight of fancy. Human beings are far from perfect. We are all at times more or less irrational, emotional, and poorly programmed. To get blind justice from that combination would need a miracle.

The self-interested person does not take the naïve attitude that just because the court process is symbolized by a blindfolded woman holding a scale, justice will be delivered. It is important to be reasonable and practical and get the best attorney you can. Learn as much as you can about the law. Make notes that will assist your lawyer and which will make your case as strong as you can precisely because justice is not blind.

'You can't legislate morality.' This is one of the most curious of all the superstitions I've come across. A quick examination will show that we behave in decent ways for three reasons. The first is that we believe it is simply right and proper to do the decent and right thing. No one needs to tell me not to shove someone into traffic, for example. I don't do that, not only because it is against the law, but also because I think it's a foolish and cruel thing to do. It's also for this same reason that I pay taxes. I feel a government needs the support of its citizens to be able to provide highways, police protection, military defence, plus thousands of other services. It also needs the income to do so. I may not enjoy paying the taxes and may not always agree with how much I'm asked to pay — but that's beside the point.

The second reason why we behave as civilized and decent people is that our religions tell us that certain behaviours are immoral. We are told, for example, that we should not steal, or commit adultery, or kill. To go against these religious teachings one risks the disapproval of one's church, as well as the feelings of guilt which usually accompany sinful behaviour. The fear of being punished by God or being sent to hell is a very powerful motive for keeping people on the straight and narrow.

17

The third reason why people behave decently is that the law places an obligation upon them to do so. It is certainly true that many of the laws we observe are concerned with behaviour which we would stick to because we feel it right and proper to do so and because it would be against our religion not to. Abusing children, for example, is not only an indecent thing to do, and against religious teachings, it is also against the law in most civilized societies. But take speeding. You might not think that driving under a prescribed speed has anything to do with decency, and you might not think it any concern of your religion, but you would still do it simply because you'd get a ticket or spend some time in jail if you didn't. A great deal of our behaviour is controlled by whether or not it is legal or illegal. If we're going to be punished with fines, loss of property or jail sentences for performing certain acts, we're certainly not inclined to perform them.

If you, as a self-interested person, are unhappy with certain behaviours in your life, then try to pass laws or rules to change them. Don't take the attitude that morality can't be legislated. Morality is frequently legislated. For example, if you don't like people smoking in your office, pass a law to stop having other people pollute your air. If you think it's wrong of landlords to throw you out of your home on the first day that you can't pay the rent, don't hesitate to support a law that allows you time to make your payment. If you think it's wrong for women to be dismissed from employment because they're pregnant, then support a law to prevent that sort of treatment.

Those and thousand of behaviours of this kind are all moral in nature because they have to do with fairness, safety, and the welfare of the people involved. Self-interested people know this. They're smart about what they have a right to expect from society and they know how to go about it. Self-negligent people don't believe this, so they go through their lives ignoring countless opportunities to improve their situation.

'It's the principle that counts.' When you want to decide whether an act is proper or improper you knowingly or

unknowingly ask yourself if it follows a given moral principle. For example, if your child steals a few pennies from your purse, you may feel perfectly justified in penalizing the child because a moral principle has been violated. This view takes the position that an act is wrong simply because it has a degree of immorality connected to it and it makes little difference whether it is a great deal of immorality or a little immorality.

I think this is wrong. What is wrong with some behaviour is not the behaviour itself but the *degree* to which it exists. If you habitually tell the truth in every detail because you believe that a little falsehood is just as bad as a big one, they you will lose friends. You believe that a lie is a lie and that the size of a lie has nothing to do with the issue. You might say the same about stealing. If stealing is bad then it doesn't matter whether a person is caught stealing one dollar or a hundred thousand. The crime is the same.

Those people who do not make this distinction are self-negligent. They treat all misbehaviours alike. One wrong is just as bad as another. Under this system justice is miscarried very blatantly. How is it that a young girl who stole five dollars could be sent to prison in Florida for five years, while at the same time company executives who defrauded the government of millions of dollars served no jail sentences at all? They were simply asked to repay the money which they misused and that was the end of that. For justice to have been carried out, the young girl should have received a lecture and the corporate executive should have been sent to jail.

'Honesty is the best policy.' To be perfectly honest and above board with people who are giving you difficulties is of course an extremely sound practice. Unless you register your complaints accurately and without apology you are not going to be able to get the other person to understand what your problem is and thereby have it solved. Honesty is unquestionably the best policy when you have conflicts with someone and you need to get a very important and disagreeable issue

settled. However, simply because it is the best policy to be honest is these situations, people take it for granted that honesty is always the best policy in practically all other situations.

I disagree. I can think of a number of instances where being honest with someone when no mighty issue hangs in the balance is simply being cruel. It is at such times that the civilized and gentle person does not clobber his loved one or his friend with brutal honesty. Let's face it, to be honest means sometimes that people will learn things that they don't need to hear. It is frequently a painful experience to face the truth. If it does no great good to face the truth then why do we have to insist upon being so honest that the truth be revealed? But what about those times when being truthful is uncivilized, impolite, and downright cruel?

If someone is dying and asks if you have any complaints against him, would you be brutally honest and express every degree of disapproval you had towards him? If you did you'd be a callous clod. What good would it do to say to your dying friend that you always thought he was a skinflint? What is to be gained by such honesty at the moment when a person is ready to leave this world?

Flattery is often a matter of telling white lies. Why be compulsively honest if a woman asks whether you like her dress or her hair? Unless it is absolutely ugly and she really needs to be told that she looks a fright, then by all means tell her it looks delightful and make her feel good. People aren't really asking for the truth in such instances in the first place. They want you to agree with their choice of clothing or with their sense of beauty. To get technical at a time like that and to tell a woman that she should have dyed her hair darker is to be no more than gauche.

When children bring their minor accomplishments to us, all smiles and with joy in their hearts, and they ask us what we think, what are we supposed to say? The parent who says of his child's painting 'Darling, that is not good art. It stinks.

You are going to have to do this many many times and take lessons before you learn how to do it properly', is simply taking the wind out of the child's sails. Honesty is not called for at a time like that. Of course a six-year-old is not going to draw a masterpiece. But so what? We don't expect the child's efforts to be outstanding and could say instead 'Oh, Jimmy, I think you are doing very well. That's so much better than I thought you could do. Keep up the good work. I especially like the way you drew that house.' This is not being untruthful, it simply ignores the fact that the drawing is probably pretty crude which hardly needs to be communicated at all.

Honesty is also not always the finest and the most sensible course of action at your place of work. If your boss is an insecure fellow and needs some agreement on a minor issue, why not go along with him? If you value your job and you know that this fellow looks for compliments, why not give him compliments? If he makes a speech and you tell him it was really great, you may be straining the truth a bit, but again, isn't that the kind of medicine he may require? He'll feel good about it, he'll appreciate you and like you for it, and everybody will get along fine. If you were to tell him in some detail how inadequate you thought his speech was, you'd probably put him on the defensive, make him like you less, and perhaps even put your job on the line.

Let us, therefore, always distinguish whether it is worth expressing one's views openly or whether one shouldn't hold back and stretch the truth a bit. That's called diplomacy. That's called charm. That's called tenderness. And that's something we don't have enough of in the world.

These are just some of many myths and superstitions which people accept blindly, to their often severe detriment. Perhaps you can think of others. Do take the time, as I have done in these previous few pages, to ask yourself whether they really make all that much sense. You may well find they don't.

Fanatical Thinking

The second major type of faulty thinking is that done by fanatics. This differs from the superstitious thinking we have just covered in that it contains a strong element of obsession. In fanactic thinking we are dealing with people who again don't examine their thoughts very carefully but who, at the same time, get so carried away with their beliefs that they take them to extremes.

People can be fanatical about religion, politics, health, money, and many other matters. If you become fanatic about money you become a miser, you spend your life accumulating money but never enjoy it because you fear losing it. If you become a health fanatic you might diet to the point of starvation and become anorexic, as many adolescents do. You might take vitamins, run a hundred miles a week, but you are so afraid of putting on a pound of fat that you ruin your health by eating like a scarecrow.

Aristotle told us that moderation is the best path to follow. This principle of not overdoing a behaviour in either direction is called the Rule of the Golden Mean and this is precisely the quality missing in fanatics.

Some fanatics, in addition to overdoing their loyalty to an idea, get all wrapped up personally with their idealistic projects in the hope that this will bring them fame or some other form of recognition. Fanatics are so desperate for attention that they gravitate to extreme causes knowing full well that these are the ones that make people sit up and take notice. In some cases it leads to consequences which are so serious and long-lasting that whatever publicity the fanatic gets hardly makes up for the pain his behaviour brings. Let's look at a few examples.

Suicidal missions. For most of us the kamikaze attacks by the

Japanese military pilots on enemy targets were probably the first modern introduction we had to this fanatical type of behaviour. A kamikaze pilot uses his aeroplane as a bomb, and deliberately flies at a target and smashes into it knowing full well that he will die in the crash. He does not expect to escape. He does this out of a sense of duty in the belief that he is a super-soldier and that his sacrifice will go down in history and never be forgotten.

The same applies to the young men who drove trucks loaded with explosives into buildings in the Lebanon. These men did not expect to live through the ordeal and they resigned themselves to martyrdom. They believed they would go to heaven and have a special place there for their fatal act.

It should come as no surprise that kamikaze pilots and terrorist drivers are mostly young men. Middle-aged people will generally see things in a more mature perspective. They are on the whole not so gullible as to believe that one heroic act can be important or will be long remembered. And even if it should be remembered for a time it can hardly do that much good. These are acts of extreme self-neglect. These martyrs are in effect telling themselves and the world that they don't value themselves as persons.

Self-immolation. The practice of committing suicide by setting fire to oneself has probably been around for centuries but is not common in modern Western culture. Most of us first became acquainted with it during the Vietnam War when the Vietnamese monks protested against the policies of their government with respect to their religious freedoms. Since then, the practice has occasionally been copied in other parts of the world.

The dynamics behind such an act are fairly understandable even though the act itself is quite bizarre. What could be more dramatic than pouring petrol on your body and setting it afire while a crowd gathers around you staring helplessly and in horror at the ghastly sight of flames consuming a human being? But how can one determine how effective such acts of protest actually are? Is it possible that these sacrifices gain their objective? Have many policies been turned around because these unhappy persons burned for their causes?

It hardly seems so to me. An unemployed young male in the United States who protested against the economic policies of the government in the early 1980s by setting himself alight in a park accomplished absolutely nothing. He was an item of news on TV and in the papers, was talked about for a short while, but was soon forgotten.

These fanatical actions go far beyond reason; they offer little in the way of reward. I find it strange that people who are made miserable with a condition should then go and be the instruments of greater distress than they are already suffering. Being unemployed is bad, but hardly as bad as being burned to death or, if one survives such an ordeal, being scarred and crippled for life. No protest is worth such a fate. Self-immolation may be the ultimate sacrifice, but it is also a supreme act of self-neglect. The brief satisfaction the martyr gains from thinking others will pity him and feel great guilt because of his suffering is very short-lived and does not achieve the spectacular ends which the victim has in mind.

Anti-war protestors. Most of the student protestors against the war with Vietnam marched and yelled and held up placards. They held rallies, made speeches, and wrote to their Congressmen. They worked in politics with church groups and used these and other methods to express their feelings. This was a group that protested in a rational manner. They didn't spend time in jail for this, they weren't usually injured, and they did little violence to others or to property.

There were a number of others, however, who bombed government buildings, university laboratories and draft boards, spilled ink or blood on draft records, and in effect became terrorist organizations. They went to extremes, as all fanatical groups do, and resorted to some of the very evils they were fighting. Some of these persons were jailed and are still in prison. While their friends and classmates have finished college, have jobs, have families, enjoy holidays, vacations, and all the blessings of normal civilian life, these poor souls are sitting in jail cells practically totally forgotten by the whole generation for which they sacrificed themselves.

Again, this is self-neglect at its worst. Few remember their names. The causes for which they made their sacrifices are history. We don't talk about them anymore. Today most people wonder what all the fuss was about. How sad it is that people have altered their lives forever over matters which have few or no consequences today. Their actions were largely flashes in the pan.

Will the fanatics ever learn? Though civil disobedience has its rightful place and has often accomplished major changes in society, there are a great many more acts of disobedience which amount to nothing but pointless and ineffectual expressions of adolescent anger which, in the long run, signify nothing.

The world needs rebels and it needs revolutions. But such movements are always risky. It's important, therefore, to separate the serious revolutionary from the fanatical revolutionary. People who are smart about life do. That's the difference between those who make wild gestures that get them a brief moment of notoriety and a lifetime of punishment, and those who are well organized, belong to wide-scale movements, and bring about meaningful change. These are leaders who later become managers, chairmen, and presidents. They are honoured in song and ceremony while the pathetic rebels who act in anger and recklessness are often punished and forgotten.

Cults. We have had religious fanatics since the beginning of civilization and they certainly haven't disappeared even in modern times. A cult is a group of people whose beliefs are vastly different from those of the more popular and organized religions. To the common observer the cult members are outside the socially accepted religious movements and practise religious beliefs which seem strange or even bizarre.

Cults can also be identified by the fact that they have a leader who sets policy and who often becomes enormously wealthy as a result of his uncritical followers working hard for him many hours a day. We need only think of Reverend Jim Jones who founded Jonestown in South America; or the Bhagwan Rajneesh, the spiritual leader of a cult once based in Oregon; the Reverend Sun Moon, who has an incredible amount of sway over his followers even to the point of being able to tell them whom they should marry and when they should divorce.

Cultists are people who seem to need a strong leader to guide them. They are people in transition, they have not realized their own adult capacities and are, therefore, still subject to the strong hand of a father-figure who will take them under his wing and love them if they obey his peculiar rules. This guarantee of security is precisely what these cultists want and this is why they sacrifice so much for it. This is why Rajneesh had over ninety Rolls Royces, aeroplanes for his personal use, and a fortune at his disposal. The Reverend Moon is also an extremely wealthy person.

The Reverend Jim Jones is an even more incredible example of how people will gravitate towards a strong figure and be convinced of the most outlandish things. We all know of the great tragedy that occurred in Jonestown, Guyana. When he told his followers to line up at the punch bowl and drink poison, they did so. You couldn't write stranger fiction.

The followers in each case of these cults have to be considered extremely self-negligent people. How else can you explain young men and women walking through our airports long hours of the day selling flowers for no personal gain? How else can we understand why the followers of another religious leader will deny themselves their own pleasures and opportunities for financial advancement and give their guru great wealth? What else are we to believe when another cult leader orders his followers to line up and drink poison and they do it by the hundreds, without question and protest?

Naïvety

This is the third kind of faulty thinking which is common in people who tend to be losers in life. By its very nature, naïvety is never evident to the naïve themselves yet so obvious to those who aren't that they have difficulty understanding it. There are several subjects about which people are extremely naïve and which almost invariably bring them discomfort, misfortune and needless pain.

Power. It is often said that power corrupts absolutely. Perhaps so. It is for this reason that some people refuse to seek power. They are therefore content to be followers. Acquiring power, they believe, would force them to be cruel and greedy.

It cannot be denied this could happen. However, does this necessarily mean that anyone who seeks power has to follow the same course? Was Abraham Lincoln drunk on power? Were Washington or Jefferson? Was there never a general who had enormous power and was able to maintain a human perspective and not take advantage of his fellow man? Of course there was.

It is time we realized that if we shun the pursuit of power we leave a vacuum for the ruthless among us to fill, and abuse of power inevitably follows. Therefore, if we feel we have a strong moral cause, then why don't *we* pursue it and struggle for it as hard as the unprincipled scoundrel does?

Out of a sense of humility and inadequacy you might protest that you do not have the ability to manage power and that you would find such a responsibility overwhelming. Perhaps you attribute god-like qualities to those who have possessed power. If so, you are grossly mistaken.

Consider why some people seek power in the first place. They feel inadequate and wish to mask these inadequacies by seeking greatness, as reflected by money, power and status, to strike down their inner doubts about their own worth.

Self-interested people take leadership with a grain of salt. They maintain a healthy degree of caution and scepticism about people who want power so much. But at the same time they are not afraid of taking power for themselves. They know that the most wretched among us are among the most powerless: minorities, children and prisoners, for example. In order to get the most out of life it is most important to have some degree of control: it is the self-negligent who give up that control to others.

Do not take pride in the fact that you are meek. It is better to be strong and use your power kindly, than to be meek and depend upon kindly power.

Wealth. Some of you have the same aversion towards acquiring wealth that you have for acquiring power. You think it is filthy, vulgar, greedy, and sinful to become rich. You look upon money as something which is always stolen from others and therefore is undeserved. You don't see wealth as one of the most convenient ways to achieve power. Yet, the moment you are short of money you wish you had some. When going for an interview in college you don't want to admit to the admission board that you want to go into medicine or business because you want to be financially comfortable. You have to say that you want to help the community, or that you want to do good for mankind. To report blatantly that you want to live the good life is simply not acceptable. You would be called a crass materialist if you expressed such sentiments, wouldn't you?

Couples who want families have to square up to the issue of whether they want to have more children than they might be able to afford. They agonize over such decisions because they feel they should not interfere with the natural process of having children in a loving marriage. It troubles them to connect love and family with mere matters of finance.

That is an uneducated, foolish and self-negligent attitude. Those people who think carefully about how much a child is going to cost them and how many children they can afford are the smart ones. They admit to themselves unashamedly that their income presently can pay for college education for their one or two children but not more. They enjoy their standard of living and do not want it reduced by the cost of another child.

They like money and the evenings out which it provides them because it is a great relief to have some variety in their lives. They enjoy going on vacation. They enjoy a new car every so often so they don't have to ride in a dangerous and unsafe one. They enjoy being able to pay their medical bills and take good care of their teeth so they can preserve their good looks. They enjoy being able to have friends and to entertain them with special meals and a fine bottle of wine. When they accept new jobs they ask themselves not only whether they'll like the work they'll be doing but also whether it will pay them enough to meet their material needs. They are materialists and they are pleased to be so. They are not totally governed by money, of course, nor the nice things that it buys. And, if they don't have to hurt others or themselves to get it, they feel good about getting it.

Most of all, they are honest with themselves. If we were to be quite honest about our feelings of wanting to live in lovely homes in nice neighbourhoods, have fine clothes, and have all the trappings that go with a reasonably comfortable income, practically everyone would pursue such an end. Poverty stinks and if you don't believe it try it sometime. Grow old before your time. Lose your teeth and your looks before you're old. Suffer with your illnesses because you can't afford to have them corrected. Freeze in your home because you can't afford fuel. Eat unbalanced meals because you can't buy the variety you need.

Money is not the root of all evil. It is the *exclusive* love of money which is wrong. If used with good sense and sound judgement, money is the root of more happiness, comfort, freedom, and personal fulfilment than almost anything else with the possible exception of one's health and ethical and spiritual values.

Education. Ignorance costs a fortune. The more education you have, the more unique you become. The more unique you become, the more money you can generally command. And if you have a skill which is widely needed, you may be able to command a better salary by taking your skills abroad.

Without education you're likely to suffer from an absence of power and an absence of wealth. This isn't always true, of course. For example a fellow can make his fortune by being a terrific tap dancer or trumpet player without ever making it beyond grade school. And his wealth will give him power and open doors that are hardly open even to the professor in the local community college. But such instances are the exception rather than the rule. In general, education makes life easier for you because it leads to a better standard of living.

But a better standard of living isn't all an education can provide. As you acquire education you don't simply accumulate information, you undergo a process of fundamental change. A certain degree of education makes you a qualitatively different kind of human being — wiser, more compassionate, curious, more interesting, and healthier than you would be without it.

I shall never forget the intellectual awakening I underwent as a postgraduate student. The four years I spent as an undergraduate were enormously important to me but they taught me more about mathematics and chemistry than about life. It wasn't until I pursued further study that I became alive as a thinking human being. I understood so much more of my world and why people behave as they do than I would have had I not had this exposure. Courses such as history, anthropology, psychology, religion, and sociology gave me an understanding of myself and others and how we reached our present situation. They taught me to be more compassionate, less biased, and more rational in my thinking.

In my view, one of the most self-negligent things you can do is not to take advantage of all the schooling you can reasonably get; to stop learning. Children are often told this by their parents and it is a great pity that so many children do not understand how important education is to them. They may not appreciate this when they are in high school because they are tired of learning; they get out so as to get a job or to marry. So many of my clients who have done this tell me it is one of their greatest regrets. It isn't until they are about thirty years of age that they often long for a life of greater freedom and fun which they can't have because they have a family and many responsibilities. And it is at this same time that they decide to complete their education, pick up a new trade, or get a professional degree because they realized ten years later than was necessary that their parents were indeed correct. How unfortunate that they learned to be self-caring a decade late.

I hope you will not misunderstand this entire discussion by thinking that power and money are the only qualities we must strive for. A reasonable amount of power and wealth are all that it generally takes to aquire a comfortable life. We can get sufficient satisfaction and security even if we don't make millions or have a yacht we can retire to. And it is absolutely true that the very wealthy or the very powerful are not always the happiest among us. But on the average, those who have a *reasonable* amount of control over their lives because they're powerful and because they have adequate incomes or education are the ones who fare better in this world than those who don't. Those are the facts of life, not conditions which I think are necessarily fair. In a perfectly fair society these qualities would probably make very little difference. But life is not fair and if you want a reasonable amount of fulfilment in this world, you had better observe the way the world actually runs.

4

Control Yourself

So far we've been almost entirely concerned with the way we use our brains. We've tried to explain why some people don't think for themselves, and we've had a look at some of the reasons for faulty thinking and what this can do to us. Many of you are perhaps prone to bouts of depression, anger or fear, and you may well think that this is something completely natural and something that 'just happens'. If so, it may well come as something of a surprise to learn that you can learn to control these neurotic emotions by using your brain. It isn't by any means easy, but it certainly can be done.

A neurotic emotion isn't something that 'just happens'. It is something you give yourself which makes your situation worse, not better, but which once you've been taught how, can be avoided. But why is it you suffer these emotions? Is it because you aren't smart? Not usually. You make things worse because you've been trained to do so, and because you're imperfect and your brain has a way of going lazy on you so that clear thinking isn't usually the result. That's why Dr Ellis defined a neurotic as a 'non-stupid person who behaves stupidly'. I have a slightly different definition: a neurotic is 'a person who takes a bad situation and makes it worse'. We're saying roughly the same thing, just focusing on different parts of the neurotic process.

When a parent spanks a child to stop him or her from crying, the child cries all the harder. When a man gives his wife the third degree because he's jealous and wants to know if she has seen someone while she was out, she loves him less, not more. When a worker shouts back at his boss because the boss showed favouritism to another employee, the man increases the chances of being passed over for another promotion someday. Though none of these people may in fact be stupid they are acting stupidly, making their frustration worse. That's what we mean by neurotic behaviour.

But wait, aren't these all examples of everyday, normal reactions? Don't *all* people do this from time to time? Yes they do. These *are* examples of normal behaviour. But so what? Just because they're normal doesn't mean they're healthy. In other words, normal behaviour is neurotic behaviour. Healthy behaviour is not. I want to teach you *not* to be normal. I want to teach you to be healthy, to be self-caring, to be good to yourself.

Frustrations and disturbances

One of the most important facts you'll need to learn if you want to control your feelings is that frustrations are not the same as disturbances. Unless you make this distinction you'll give yourself endless stress, headaches, tantrums, or bad nerves.

Let's illustrate the distinction by means of an example. You are waiting in the rain for a taxi. That's uncomfortable; that's a frustration. As you wait in the rain for the taxi, you get angry. That's an emotional disturbance. The two are related not *directly* but *indirectly*. It isn't the frustration of standing in the rain that causes you to get angry. Frustrations do not cause emotional disturbances. You don't have to get angry. You *choose* to get angry. That's what I mean when I say that frustrations are not the same as emotional disturbances.

Not convinced? Are you finding it hard to believe that nothing can upset you unless you allow it to? Then let me ask you if everyone who waits in the rain gets mad. Of course they don't. And haven't you noticed how on one day you're not upset at all when a salesgirl treats you rudely, but on another day you're very upset? How you can react differently to the same event if the event determines the reaction?

Well then, if our emotional reactions are not determined by frustrations, what does cause us to be depressed, angry, fearful, or to procrastinate? The answer will surprise you. It is your thoughts *about* your frustrations. Your *thoughts* determine your feelings, your frustrations themselves do not.

This means you must be very careful of how you think, lest you develop strong neurotic patterns. If you think sensibly, logically and rationally, you'll be annoyed, impatient, and irritable perhaps, but you won't be depressed, angry, or jealous (which are far more intense emotions). However, if you think carelessly, illogically, and irrationally, you'll get upset every time.

Rational Emotive Therapy

Simply put, emotional disturbances are caused by the thoughts we have when we feel frustrated. Dr Albert Ellis in formulating his theory of Rational Emotive Therapy, identified eleven irrational beliefs which cause us to feel such conditions as depression, pity, guilt, inferiority, anger, hate, fury, fear, worry, nervousness, panic, jealousy, possessiveness, passivity, procrastination, and other forms of escape. The precise feelings you will suffer will be determined by the precise irrational thoughts you have.

To reduce or rid yourself of these painful conditions you need to train yourself to reject these irrational ideas, to question their soundness so completely that you no longer think they make sense. That requires hard work and practice — and lots of it. All of this sounds simple to explain but don't think for one moment that it's all that easy to talk yourself out of disturbances when you've probably been practising the habit of upsetting yourself ever since you were a child.

Eleven irrational ideas and their rational analyses

Irrational Idea no.1. *Being unloved or disapproved of proves you are bad and worthless. Rejection hurts. You have value only if people important to you regard you highly. If they respect and/or love you, then you are an acceptable human being.*

Nonsense! Why and how does someone's rejection turn you into an evil, rotten, or worthless person? Who are they to pass judgement anyway? Are they perfect? Besides, rejection does not hurt unless you let it hurt. It's unpleasant and sad, to be sure, but hardly the end of the world.

Irrational Idea no.2. *Behaving badly, stupidly, or immorally makes you a bad and worthless person. Only if you are outstanding, a high achiever and nearly perfect can you think well of yourself. Mistakes are terrible and prove how bad you really are.*

Since when? The only way any of us can ever be free of errors is when we're dead. All other living people will make mistakes — millions of them — as long as they live. If imperfect people are no good, then every person who ever lived, who is presently alive, or who will ever live is bad, rotten, evil, and worthless.

Irrational Idea no.3. *There are bad and wicked people in the world and blaming or punishing them severely will cure them of this evil. Screaming, beating, torture, and attacking the person's personality are all good methods to achieve emotional growth.*

Rubbish! People and their behaviour are not the same. We cannot logically conclude that bad behaviour makes a bad person since the same people perform many, many behaviours, some bad or cruel, but some wonderful and kind.

Instead of putting people down or abusing them physically, let's finally admit that these ancient methods don't work well at all, and even when they do, the cost to the person's future health is enormous. For example, a tough teenager might be brought to submission if he were flogged routinely and then kept in solitary confinement. But what kind of a person would you have left?

Irrational Idea no.4. *It is awful and catastrophic when you don't get your way. Life should be fair. And if you're right you certainly deserve to get everything you're entitled to. Not to get your way is unbearable.*

Wrong again. You *never* need to have your way. The world was not made to suit your particular preferences. Not getting your way is irritating, annoying, and sad, but not horrible, terrible or so awful you can't tolerate it. What, pray tell, do you plan to do instead? Not tolerate it? To do that you'd have to die. That's the only way to guarantee not putting up with something you don't like. Therefore, if you're not ready to die, then you'll have to tolerate your frustrations until you can reduce or remove them, or put up with them until, and if, they pass.

Irrational Idea no.5. *Emotional disturbance and human unhappiness are caused by the events in our lives and this leaves us with little or no control over our disturbances. People, in other words, make us depressed, angry, jealous, etc. If we want to get rid of these emotional pains we must get others to stop treating us so badly.*

Not so! No one upsets you but yourself. People frustrate you. You disturb yourself. By talking ourselves into believing that our disturbances come from outside of ourselves we can readily blame everyone and his brother for our emotional sufferings. It's about time we were honest with ourselves and admitted the truth — that we talk ourselves into getting upset one day and talk ourselves out of being upset the next. We are in charge of our emotions. If we're rational with ourselves we're in good shape. If we're irrational, we're in trouble.

Irrational Idea no.6. *We should be very concerned about dangerous or threatening situations, and we should worry and focus endlessly upon them. Worrying guards against surprises and guarantees that the problems won't get worse.*

On the contrary. The more you worry and go over a thought, the more nervous you'll feel. And, you will not have done a thing about the threat you are so concerned about.

Challenge the idea repeatedly that dwelling and focusing on problems and frustrations is helpful. Paying *some* attention to your problems always makes sense. However, when you get *more* upset rather than less upset from focusing on a problem, you're overdoing a good thing.

Irrational Idea no.7. *It is easier to avoid difficult situations than it is to face them. Then you get instant relief, and, because life is short, hard work doesn't always pay off. So why not play first and get to the unpleasant chores later?*

Because it's easier in the long run, that's why. It is not the undisciplined people who have the best of life, it's the disciplined. The procrastinators are the ones who usually enjoy the brief pleasures only to complain later about all the headaches they must endure because they didn't face the hard duties first.

Practically all skills and rewards come from hard work. You didn't get through school by staying in bed every morning, or not doing homework. If you did squeak by, you cheated yourself of an education.

The real winners are those who did the tough work first and then enjoyed their rewards later. That's why they are so well off — they saved their money and then invested it; they studied hard and got a well-paid job, they exercised and dieted wisely and they're healthy and young-looking for it.

Fooling around is easy on you for only a short while. It gets its pound of flesh later. Facing problems is hard on you at first, for a few minutes or hours or days, but then, for months or years you reap enormous rewards.

Irrational Idea no.8. *It is better to rely on people who are stronger or more powerful than you if you want to feel secure. They know how to make smart decisions. They have connections and money which can help you when in trouble. Having all this going for you will make you feel as secure as a child with a millionaire or a king for a father.*

On the contrary. The more you rely on others the less you

will rely on yourself. What do you think will happen to you if the one you rely on dies, or dislikes you, or moves away? That leaves you bereft, like an orphan. Your hero and benefactor will learn to be very responsible if you refuse to make decisions and risk errors. He or she will become quite skilled at thinking through tough problems and making choices.But you will still remain frightened of mistakes.

Ask yourself how the person you lean on became so skilled and reliable in the first place. Why is he or she so able and comfortable at taking charge, ordering from a menu, deciding which purchase to make? It is mostly because that person has done it over and over again and learned from the school of hard knocks. If you want the same skills, stick your neck out, take responsibility and risk occasionally being wrong. That's how you too can learn to be big and strong psychologically just like the person you now lean on.

Irrational Idea no.9. *Whatever you experienced years ago has got to influence you today and leave you quite powerless to fight against those childhood forces. You are programmed by millions of events and what you are today is what you were trained to be over the many years of growing up. And some of those things you learned at your mother's feet can never be unlearned.*

Since when? If life is anything, it is a learning experience. What was learned can be unlearned. If you were trained to be shy or aggressive, humble or ambitious, insecure or self-confident, you can change the former into the latter or vice versa. The choice is yours. Thank your good fortune that this is so, for otherwise you would have to behave like a robot who is programmed one way and cannot change. Life teaches us all, and most of the time you and I rethink our beliefs and change accordingly. When this is particularly difficult to do because we have been deeply conditioned (with fear or anger), psychotherapy may be necessary to bring about changes in old beliefs.

Irrational Idea no.10. *We should be upset and disturbed over other people's problems. It's only natural to get upset over the suffering of others. To do otherwise is a sign of cold-blooded heartlessness. Caring people feel what others feel, to the same degree.*

Hopefully not. If you break your heart over someone else's heartbreak, you are adding more misery to the world, not less. In addition, you will not be in a good position to assist those you are so hurt over.

Would you want a surgeon to anguish over your suffering and lose his concentration? Would you want a minister to identify and feel for your depression so much that he too experiences a severe depression? The counsellor who suffers along with each of his clients will be in no shape to return to the office the next day.

What we all want are people who *care* about the suffering of the unfortunate, not who *overcare*. This is the same point I have made before: it is appropriate to be sad without feeling tragic, to be annoyed rather than furious, and to be alert and careful rather than panicky.

Irrational Idea no.11. *All problems have one and only one perfect solution. It is foolish to act on a problem until you are certain your solution is the perfect one. Until you know for certain how to deal correctly and precisely with an issue you must wait patiently, labour, search, and ask. When you are sure you are correct, then and only then should you act.*

Don't you wish! Life would be so much easier if there were one right answer to each problem and that we could identify it once we encountered it. No such luck. Life is a matter of probabilities. There are many roads to Rome. Until we examine them all, we will not know which is the shortest.

In any event, rather than avoid taking reasonable action until we are certain, we are likely to spend so much time looking for perfection that often the discovery comes too late. I believe it is far more sensible to act with a reasonable expectation of success than to delay until you are certain. In addition, even then there is no way of being certain you have come upon the completely right and precise solution.

So take chances, as long as they are based on careful planning and reasonable study.

Those of you who refuse to confront these irrational beliefs will continue going through life being enormously self-negligent. Stop doing this to yourself. Learn how you hurt yourself emotionally. Learn how to reduce or even stop some of the most common emotional disturbances. It's possible at last. We now know enough about human behaviour that this is a reasonable goal for mankind.

In the following pages I will explain the dynamics of the most common emotional problems I encounter daily in my practice and which people want me to lecture on in my seminars. They are: depression; anger; fear; procrastination; and jealousy.

Depression

Depression seems to be caused by three irrational attitudes: self-hate, self-pity, and other-pity.

Self-hate

If you do not want to get depressed again, practically for the rest of your life, then never hate yourself again. You do not have to be without fault to be an acceptable person. Always separate your behaviour from yourself and acknowledge the fact that you are guilty of an error or some misconduct without at the same time hating yourself. Whatever the behaviour, unless you do this you will feel guilty, inferior and depressed, without fail.

It is my contention that you have the right and the obligation to forgive yourself for anything. Whatever bad thing you did was done for one of three reasons and for which you have a right to forgive yourself. First, you might have been *deficient* and unable to do something correctly, such as grasp a mathematical problem, play a musical instrument, or to be patient with your children. Not all of us are born with those abilities. So how can we hate ourselves for lacking a talent we had little control over?

Second, you may *not have been taught* to do something correctly even though you may have the ability. Mothers and fathers often hate themselves for mistakes they make as parents even though they may never have had experience as parents. But how can they expect to get everything right first time? To err is human. They'll know a good deal more about childrearing when they have their second, third, and fourth child. Isn't that the way it ought to be? If you hate yourself for being a bad parent, you will destroy your self-confidence and probably make the same errors again.

Third, you have a right and an obligation to forgive yourself if you do something when *highly disturbed*. After all, there is no way you can be fully rational when very upset. If you do not know how not to be disturbed, then how can you always be a calm and collected person?

Self-pity

The world is often cruel and people are often unjust. Our greatest efforts are frequently left unappreciated. It is not uncommon to allow such inconsiderate events to hurt our feelings. The depression in this case is caused by self-pity. Whether you put yourself out greatly for someone and the favour was never returned, or whether someone close to you has moved away, it is not uncommon to feel sorry for yourself over these sad events.

Feeling sad is one thing, however. It is a normal and sensible reaction to some of the unfortunate things that happen to us. We have no quarrel with feeling sad, disappointed, or regretful. But it is an emotional and philosophical leap to go from feeling sad about something to feeling depressed. If you pity yourself and then suffer a genuine depression because of this unfair world, you are again doing what I said at the beginning of this chapter not to do when we come face to face with frustration. We tend to make it ten times worse. You can feel sorry for yourself if you want to, but you would be so much better off to count your blessings and to realize that things could be worse.

This is the way people have endured unfairness, injustice, deprivation, and poverty for thousands of years. They have convinced themselves that things may be bad but still be grateful for the fact that they aren't any worse. Self-pity comes from Irrational Idea no.4, that we must have every-thing we want and that it is terrible and awful if life doesn't treat us as we wish. Challenge that idea and you will not suffer self-pity.

Other-pity

To feel concern and compassion for another person's suffer-ing is the mark of civility. You are concerned over others, you care for and do favours for them, and you feel you are your brother's keeper. And so it should be. When things go wrong for those we care for, and for mankind in general, we are behaving in magnificent and mature ways when we show that we are interested beyond our own immediate concerns. And when unfortunate things happen we wisely allow ourselves to become somewhat unhappy, pensive, sad, and uneasy.

Those again are normal emotional reactions. What you must avoid are the *extreme* emotional reactions to other people's misfortunes, to believe that what happened was a horrible, terrible, or earth-shattering and catastrophic ex-perience.It is not true that most of the things you worry about and get depressed over are all end-of-the-world events, matters of life and death. Most of the things we are depressed over are everyday, regrettable and disappointing events. Therefore, let us feel disappointment and regret, not depression, not despair, not desperation. Challenge Irrational Idea no.10.

There you have the way to avoid depression. Never hate yourself, because you have a right to be imprfect. Never feel sorry for yourself, you don't have to have all you want just because you think you deserve it. The world is unfair. Never feel sorry for others. Only feel concern and care. There is no sense in getting yourself greatly disturbed over someone's problems. What they need is your help. If you have an emotional breakdown, that would only be a hindrance.

Anger

This is one of the worst emotional disturbances because it expresses itself in violence, hatred, hostility, war and torture. It also expresses itself in lesser ways such as resentment, bitterness, jealously, fault-finding, nagging, and destructive criticism. In the next few pages I will teach you how to control your anger 90 per cent of the time for the rest of your life *if you work hard at it*.

The first point you must understand is that it is you who create your own anger. No one else does. You talk yourself into it and it is up to you to talk yourself out of it. How? You get angry in the first place by thinking you *must* have everything you want. You believe at that point that it is awful and horrible if you don't get everything you want and that people who frustrate you are bad, and wicked and should be hated for their wickedness (Irrational Idea no.4). You are, according to Dr Ellis, wrong on all counts. People who think they should have everything they want are just full of prunes. Just because other people frustrate you hardly makes them evil and horrible human beings who have to be criticized, beaten or killed.

Anger, then, starts by your wanting, wishing, and desiring something. But before you know it you have changed your

44

mental state (whether you realize it or not) and you convinced yourself instead that you *must have* what you want. In other words, you have changed your healthy and natural wishes and desires into neurotic needs and demands. Now remember this point: if you don't get what you want you only become disappointed and regretful. That is not serious and happens to us throughout our lives. How many of you have wanted to be rich, famous, beautiful, have a yacht on the Riviera, or have a new fur coat? And how many of you got furious and angry with the world because you didn't get those things simply because you wanted them? Obviously only a very few of you.

Now, when you convince yourself that you *have* to have something and don't get it, that's a different story. Then you become hostile, furious, bitter, resentful, and you want to hurt everyone around you or scream your head off. But don't you see what caused the anger? It is not the fact that you did not get what you wanted. It is the fact that you *thought* you *had to have* something you wanted.

Look at it this way. You have undoubtedly seen children throw tantrums. Why do they do this? Obviously because they don't get what they think they have to have. Isn't that why a four-year-old child screams, kicks, fusses, and bangs his head on the floor?

What's the difference between what this child is doing and what you are doing? There's only one difference: the kinds of frustration. The child gets disturbed over not getting a lollipop or an ice-cream cone, whereas you wanted a pay raise, or more respect, or to win at a sports event.

In other words you have adult concerns, desires, and needs. But when you get angry you are regressing to the level of a child and are behaving like a child. Aren't you above that kind of foolish and infantile behaviour? I would certainly hope so. I know it is one of the things I continually have to remind myself of whenever I find myself frustrated and am about to become angry. I immediately say to myself: 'I am not a child. I don't have to have everything I want. People who are frustrating me really aren't bad, they're simply mistaken or have some pretty strong views of their own which don't agree with mine. That hardly means they are bad or ought to be severely punished. It just means that I am going to be frustrated and not get my way. So what? I am not a baby and I *can* stand it.' When I talk to myself that way I don't get angry. You can easily do the same.

My suggestion to you angry people is to learn how to keep your mouths shut. Think it over very clearly before you explode and ask yourself why you must have everything you want even though you are perfectly deserving of them. Being right or being deserving are irrelevant. If this were heaven you would get everything you ever wanted. This is not heaven. It is earth, and sometimes the deserving and the decent simply don't get what they deserve.

And don't bring up the argument of righteous anger. All anger is righteous or you wouldn't be furious or resentful in the first place. The person you're arguing with thinks the same righteous nonsense you do. So never use that argument, it simply doesn't hold water.

Fear

There are three irrational ideas that create fear. The first is that something makes you feel afraid (Irrational Idea no.5). Everyone believes, for example, that heights, animals, skiing, scuba diving, or the possibility of injury literally make you fearful. They do not. Animals can scratch and bite, falling off heights can kill you, skiing can break your leg or paralyse you, and so forth. But it would not be accurate to say that, because you can be injured, you must be afraid. You are facing the possibility of being injured practically all day long every day of your life. But you aren't necessarily afraid to sleep in a house that has a gas furnace which could blow up on you. You don't always panic whenever you get into an elevator, cross the street, or board an aeroplane. Some people get terrified over these daily activities and others don't. What is the difference? They are both experiencing the same events and yet some are frightened, nervous, or worried, while others take the whole experience relatively calmly. The difference is in the beliefs held by the respective persons.

Whenever I have pointed this out to my clients in the past they have scoffed. The idea that one does not have to be afraid of lions, for example, is not one that many of them would accept readily. Some time ago I read in *Psychology Today* magazine about a European animal trainer who was attacked a number of times by his animals and had over five hundred stitches. Even this could not make him afraid of going back into the ring with his animals.

The second reason we become fearful lies in our belief that something is unbearable (Irrational Idea no.4). We repeatedly think this way when getting a bad grade, getting a divorce, losing a job, or being rejected by those who are dear to us. These are all uncomfortable and unfortunate events in our lives to be sure, but they are not horrible, terrible, unbearable, or catastrophic. Yet it is our neurotic belief that if unpleasant things happen to us, it is not just unfortunate, it is the end of the world. When we talk to ourselves in these catastrophic terms and believe that things are terrible, awful, horrible, or unbearable we are bound to become very upset. Instead, let us become *normally* concerned, irritated, and frustrated. That is a big improvement over being afraid, nervous, and worried.

The third way we become afraid and nervous happens when we believe the irrational idea that if something bad might happen, we should focus and dwell upon the possibility of its occurring (Irrational Idea no.6). Thus we create neurotic feelings for ourselves where none existed. We believe, if we focus endlessly on what could happen, that somehow that will prevent the event from happening. On the contrary, very often the more we worry about something the more likely it is to happen. For example, if you are giving a speech and you worry about forgetting your lines, then you are not paying attention to the speech and are more likely to forget what you are supposed to say.

If you want control over most of your fears, first, don't believe that other things make you upset. Second, stop saying that everything is a catastrophe when it is actually only a regrettable annoyance. And third, don't think that just because something is going to be uncomfortable you should think about it all the time. That will only make it worse.

Now what about those anxiety attacks? Sometimes people get very nervous over a frightening event. The danger may pass but they don't seem to forget just how upset they were during the time that they were nervous. They feel as though they were out of control, like something funny was happening to them which they did not understand. Some have even felt they might have been losing their minds and perhaps were beginning to suffer a serious emotional breakdown.

Then, if later, they have a nervous feeling or a worry passes through their minds, the thought occurs to them that perhaps they are having another one of those strange and scary feelings. Then they worry about that. And of course this is precisely what brings on another panic attack, and another, sometimes many times a day. They believe that it is a catastrophe if they have another anxiety attack even when there is no proof that it is catastrophic at all. It is certainly not a pleasant experience, but it is not an intolerable one. It is unpleasant, but it is not deadly. And lastly, just because they may have another anxiety attack hardly means that they have to think about it and worry over it all the time.

Procrastination

Most people do not regard procrastination as a major emotional disturbance. That is because it doesn't hurt at once. Procrastination feels wonderful at first because we have given into a temptation and enjoyed it thoroughly. That movie you went to may have been a lot of fun but you didn't get your term paper finished. Now you have to burn the midnight oil, do a poor job of it and hastily submit an inferior product. So your grades suffer, your career suffers. Perhaps, if you make a habit of this, you'll even drop out of school and alter the whole direction of your life. How many more examples could one easily give to demonstrate the dangers in avoiding one's responsibilities!

I find that people who get what they want have much better control over self-discipline than people who are usually complaining about life. You see, mastery over procrastination is a matter of self-discipline. If you don't know how to discipline yourself you are not in control of yourself. Every silly whim you get drives you off into a new direction and you forget what you are about. How can you conceivably travel from one point to another if you are going to be side-tracked every time you see something interesting along the road? If you know where you're going, and you discipline yourself to stick to the task, you're likely to reach your goal. And the reason why people allow themselves to be side-tracked or to delay their goals is that they don't know the secrets — the simple rules that make for good self-discipline. The five simple facts which you must observe if you want to be a self-disciplined person and to get the best out of your talents are as follows:

First, it is easier to face difficult tasks than to avoid them. Very seldom does time simply cure a bad situation if you do nothing about it. Your dishes don't get done because you watch television. You don't become a good tennis player by not practising. You don't lose weight if you don't exercise. In short, if something is difficult to do, it is easier to do it than not to do it. Parents will frequently avoid confronting their children because they know they are going to have to face another ugly scene. So they don't reprimand the child for coming in late, or for answering back, or for fighting with their brothers and sisters. And because parents would rather avoid that next quarrel they keep quiet and the problem only gets worse.

Second, it is more important to do than to do well. If you believe (as most of us have been taught) that if it's worth doing, it's worth doing well, or if you can't do it right, don't do it at all, then you have been blinded by an absurdity. Stop and think how ridiculous those statements are. For example, if the baby doesn't walk well, should the baby stop walking? Should a budding piano student stop playing the piano because he or she doesn't play the piano well? Would you ever have continued to dance if you judged your dancing by your first few efforts? Practically everything you've ever done you did badly at the first time of asking, then you got better only because you kept doing it badly for a long time.

I maintain that it is much better to do things poorly, and even badly in some cases, than not at all. The salesman who thinks he is going to do a bad job in approaching his next customer may very well do badly, but at least he can learn by his poor performance and perhaps improve it as time goes by. Whatever happened to practice?

Third, break a big task into small ones. How many times did you find yourself getting bored with what you were doing? And how many times did you insist that you couldn't undertake a task because you didn't have enough time to do it? Both of these questions arise because you don't take a particular problem and reduce it to a series of smaller problems. If you did you would be able to do a great deal more and do it in a more leisurely fashion. This is one of those gems of insight regarding good self-discipline which a lot of people have never mastered.

If you want to get a big job done, do it a little bit at a time. I guarantee you won't get bored; you take the extra time necessary to see how you are coming along and to review your work, and more importantly, you get it done. All of us have thought we needed a whole day to clean out our garages and then found upon closer examination it only took two hours.

Every writer says what he really needs is six months locked up in a log cabin miles from anywhere in order to finish that great novel. What he needs is about thirty minutes a day during which time he can nibble away at a task. In half a year he will probably have the thing done. This is exactly how I have written most of my books.

Fourth, reward yourself constantly. Behaviour which is not rewarded is usually not continued. If you want to stay with a task you have to give yourself the pat on the back which is necessary to keep you going. If other people are not rewarding you then there is no reason why you can't reward yourself. You can literally do this by giving yourself a material reward such as a good meal out, an evening out at the movies, or an article of clothing. Or you could give yourself psychological rewards, such as praise. Whatever they are, let them be small, if appropriate, and let them be frequent. And even if you are not making apparent progress, at least reward yourself for not giving up.

Finally, post-mortem: whenever you do something correctly, take the time to analyse what you did right so that you can do it again. And whenever you do something wrong, take the time to ask yourself what it was that was wrong so that you can avoid that mistake in the future. That's what a post-mortem is: you analyse your behaviour after it is done, you don't spend time whipping yourself mentally, you simply learn from what you have done and you try to improve upon it. The more time you spend hating yourself the less time you give to learning what you did wrong. If you want to profit from your experience, examine your experience.

Humiliating yourself over your low levels of success will reduce your success still further. Remember, you're never failing as long as you're trying. You only fail when you stop trying. Winners make mistakes just as losers do. In fact, they make more mistakes. The distinguishing characteristic between the two, I believe, is that a winner will not waste energy and time hating himself for his mistakes or feeling guilty for them. And he doesn't fear trying again. Winners learn by mistakes.

I marvel at times how difficult it is for some people to grasp this point. We have all known friends or family members who repeatedly react foolishly to similar situations. A person can experience a series of divorces, all for the same reason, and not have the slightest understanding as to why they are happening. No time is ever taken to ask the simple questions, 'What am I doing? What is wrong with my approach? What could I do differently next time?' These and similar questions are essential if we are going to change our mistakes and achieve ever-increasing levels of success.

How do you know when you are falling into this trap and ready to make another error as you have a dozen times before? There are several ways.

First, the moment anything goes wrong, get into the habit of taking an inventory, an honest one, by yourself, and admit whatever you think might have been at fault. Don't wait until you are fired from three jobs before you ask yourself what your problem might be. Do it the very first time. If you run out of gas, even once, ask yourself how that could happen. Just don't observe the fact, and then go about getting a tank of gas and carry on as if nothing had happened. You have gained nothing by such an observation. You need to ask yourself why you didn't observe the fact that the gas tank was low. You were probably looking at it numerous times already and you didn't notice it. So, why shouldn't that happen again? And it can do so very easily.

One of my most successful and intelligent colleagues repeatedly locked himself out of his own car. This man was no fool, but in this respect he was self-negligent. He made no attempt whatever to understand why he locked himself out the first, second, and third time. Isn't that ridiculous? It certainly wouldn't take a genius to figure out that he could easily have carried an additional key in his pocket, or tried to remind himself that he must always lock the door from the outside with his key rather than to lock the door from the inside and then slam the door shut. He certainly had the money to buy a model which required that the door be locked from the outside and couldn't be shut by pushing down the plunger and then closing the door.

The second reason people don't learn is that they react emotionally to their mistakes rather than rationally. It is simply very easy to get involved in yelling and fault-finding and to miss the vital point that a lesson is there to be learned, and the sooner everybody takes the time to think and ask the right questions the sooner those mistakes will be avoided in the future.

Another reason why we do not learn is that we are so busy justifying a mistake instantly after making it. Unless you are willing to admit that you made a mess of something there isn't anything you can do to change it. Change can usually only follow when you realize that you have a fault and that you had better improve yourself. Then you can change it. It is the insecure people, the losers again, who simply cast about whenever an error has occurred to find out what and whom they can blame. The fault lies with the tools, the weather, or someone else. Or, if by chance, these are the faults, then they had still better do exactly as I have advised and continue to ask themselves what they intend to do about the tools, or weather, or the persons involved. The problem will still exist unless they change. Sounds simple doesn't it? And it is simple to comprehend. But don't think for a moment that it is easy to do.

Jealousy

Jealousy is perhaps the most blatantly self-defeating type of behaviour considered in this chapter. Jealous people may want their loved ones to love them so badly that they drive them away with the greatest efficiency imaginable. They smother them, scream at them, make prisoners of them, forbid them the slightest pleasures, and all the while they insist they want to be loved. How can any sane person enjoy being a prisoner of jealousy and possessiveness?

I know of a woman whose husband was furious when she tried to entertain her children from her first marriage, when she had her parents over for Sunday dinner, and even when she answered the telephone or the front door. She was not to entertain her friends, nor was she to talk to anyone he did not approve of, and she practically had to walk with her eyes to the ground. And yet he expected her to love him.

I never met this gentleman but I could hardly imagine he was so blind as not to realize down deep in his heart that he was seriously injuring a lovely relationship. Surely he must have seen time after time that he was building a greater distance between himself and his wife. She was an unhappy bird in a gilded cage and if she had had the slightest bit of self-confidence and common sense she would never have put up with that nonsense in the first place.

Here are the three mistakes jealous people make. First, they think they are inferior individuals. They are afraid that anyone their loved ones talk to is a threat. They feel they must be the best, and the only ones their husbands, wives, or lovers speak to or enjoy. In effect they are saying, 'I'm no good. I cannot understand why you love me, and I know that if you become the slightest bit acquainted with anyone else, you are going to prefer that person over me.'

Second, they believe that because they are inferior (if only in certain ways) they will be rejected for that weakness. But where is the proof for this? If they would only ask themselves whether they are rejecting their partners for the same reason, they would see how irrational such a view is. Do they reject their mates because they are not the best looking, richest, most successful, or the brightest? Hardly!

And third, they believe that rejection would be unbearable and final proof of one's worthlessness. But it is vital to realize that rejection is not that painful, is not proof of worthlessness, and can be survived. In short, people do not *need* the love of their partners. They think their value as a person comes only from being loved or approved of, and that if they are not loved, they are nothing. They go by the title of that song 'You're nobody till somebody loves you'. Was there ever a more neurotic song title in history? Rejection hurts only if you make it hurt. When you get over the idea that the love someone shows you makes you or breaks you, you won't be so scared of the fact that maybe you are not the greatest lover or the best dancer, or the best mate. And you don't have to be. As long as you are able to satisfy your partner to a reasonable degree, just as your partner often satisfies you only to a reasonable degree, your relationship is safe. Once you begin to become extreme about having to be loved you begin to worry neurotically about holding onto that person. And, of course, the harder you try to control your lover, the quicker you lose your lover.

I can prove this by making two points. First, what happens to you if your lover dies, or is sent to jail for fifty years, or is inducted into the army and sent overseas? Would you not be able to survive? And second, what do you think happens to people when they drive away their husbands or wives? They don't die. They don't go crazy. They just get upset, and after a time, they find another lover. Sometimes they marry fairly quickly because they are desperate to be needed by someone. Yet, all along they had been saying they could not possibly exist and enjoy life or tolerate not being loved by the person whom they had driven from them.

Winners do not make other people *that* important in their lives. They still have self-respect and are not threatened when their partners talk to others. They relax when they go to parties and that makes them fun to be with. And because they make good company, the last thing in the world their partners want to do is to leave them.

Therefore, if you are jealous, I suggest that you keep quiet about it. Don't give your partner the third degree and make yourself a pain in the neck. Instead, let your partner enjoy the company of others. In that way they will have a good time and enjoy being with you all the more. And why should anyone want to give you up when you're such a nice person to be with? That is how smart people conduct themselves. Jealous people are self-negligent; self-caring people are not.

So control yourself. Remember that you don't have to waste your energy on anger and recriminations. If you develop your self-control and discipline you will find, in time, that you value yourself more as a person.

5

Enough Is Enough

Can you guess which single problem I deal with most frequently? Is it teaching parents new child-rearing methods? No. Is it helping the unemployed reduce their depressions? No. Or is it counselling couples to improve their sex lives? Again no. And it's not poor study habits, or shyness, alcoholism or drug abuse. It's *excessive passivity*.

Some of the problems I have just mentioned, and a great many others, are directly or indirectly related to this extremely widespread condition. Many parents would like to know how to deal with their disrespectful teenage children who won't tidy up their rooms, help with chores, or come home before curfew. They have lost control of their children and are actually afraid to put pressure on them to be co-operative.

Men and women complain repeatedly that they are taken advantage of by relatives, even parents, by friends and by people at work. The most frequent complaint comes from women who feel dominated by members of the family, especially by their husbands. Sometimes men complain about being abused and not appreciated by their wives, but they are very few compared to the number of women who flock to counsellors to seek help for feelings of anger, depression, heartbreak, and fear for their safety. Women are the most passive and abused group I encounter in my work. They are modern-day slaves, who often work incredibly hard to please their families and end up feeling exhausted and crushed.

More and more of these women are refusing to accept their condition. They don't have to. Times have changed since their mothers and grandmothers suffered economic hardship which left them no alternative but to submit to their situation or risk being thrown out on to the street because they didn't have a man to provide for them. Today, with women getting their own paycheques, the need to keep quiet has evaporated. So they read *Ms* magazine, join support groups, and go to counselling to help them cope with marriages they are losing interest in. They don't want separations or divorces. Even if they can support themselves today far better than their mothers could, they still want to preserve the love they have but are losing. And I want that for them, too.

I sincerely hope you men who are reading this book will not accuse me of taking sides. I'm not. I'm fully aware that there are plenty of immature and inconsiderate women who take shameful advantage of their hard-working husbands. And my heart goes out to them when they want my help. Injustice is blind. Both men and women suffer from manipulation and the thoughtlessness of others. And the reason is always the same: self-neglect.

What I will teach you in this chapter applies to anyone who suffers from excessive passivity. Let there be no misunderstanding about this: standing up for your rights to a sensible degree is one of the most important things you can do if you care about your happiness *and* the happiness of those around you. Be a wimp, a super nice guy, or a humble, grovelling altruist if you like, but do so at your own risk. There are many times in our lives when we all have to back down before a real threat. However, there are many more times in our lives when we don't, when standing up to unacceptable behaviour is proper, ethical, in keeping with religious teachings, and just plain healthy.

I want to teach you in this book, just as I teach my clients daily in my offices or as I teach whole audiences at lectures or seminars, that psychology has become very sophisticated during the past thirty years and is fully capable of teaching people to stand tall, to assert themselves, and dignify their lives with behaviours that make others co-operate with them rather than dominate them.

To do this you will have to learn the psychology of assertion and the psychology of emotional disturbances. Unless you learn the latter you won't be able to achieve the former. When you accomplish these two lessons and practice Rational Emotive Therapy (see Chapter 4) while you make important decisions, you'll do something important for yourself: you'll stop neglecting yourself. Decide now — this moment — that your life is about to change and change significany. Enough is enough!

Co-operation, respect and love

The degree of happiness and contentment we feel is strongly correlated to the degree of co-operation, respect and love we get from others. Self-interested people know full well that they must be co-operative, respectful and loving towards others in order to be more important to them. But they also know that they themselves need the co-operation, respect and love of others in order to remain happy and contented. To encourage others to be more co-operative, respectful and loving towards you there are three rules you should follow which I have adapted from Clifford and Charles Madsen, both PhD clinical psychologists.

Rule no.1: *If people do something nice to you, do something nice to them.*

Rule no.2: *If people do something bad to you, do something nice to them anyway, but only twice.*

Rule no.3: *If people continue to treat you badly, and talking to them has not helped, then do something equally annoying to them, but do it without anger, guilt, pity, or fear of rejection or injury.*

Rule no.1 is a common-sense reinforcement principle which we have all seen to operate so effectively in teaching our children and pets to be co-operative, respectful and loving. Each time we reinforce a good act, it grows stronger. The stronger it becomes the more likely it is to be repeated. When we are nice to others because they are nice to us, we are saying with our actions that we appreciate what has been done for us. This cannot but help others be more decent to us. Lovers find proof of their partner's deep feelings in how one act of affection is met with another. Nothing is more effective in convincing others that you care.

Rewarding others for their good behaviour is among the simplest yet most beneficial of all acts. It often costs us nothing more than a kind word or gesture. Yet we are misers in giving praise, comfort and encouragement. Instead we find fault with the greatest of ease and speak out before it even occurs to us to look for something nice to say.

Do yourself a favour and begin getting people to like you. The nicer you are to them the nicer they'll *usually* be to you. So why not endear yourself to your family, friends and co-workers by encouraging them to continue treating you well by treating them well yourself? Thank your wife for that special meal she made for you. Thank your husband for fixing the lawn mower. Thank your child for hanging up his jacket when he comes home and for tidying up his room. Give flowers, chocolates, an evening out at the movies, a vacation trip, or whatever, if it pleases the person whose co-operation, respect or love you seek. It makes no difference whether you think these rewards are trivial. Give them anyway if they please the other person. Maybe roses will fade in a few days, and maybe you think they're a waste of money. Think what you will, but don't be self-negligent and don't forget Rule no.1. If the other person thinks it's a reward, it's a reward.

But if someone does something bad to you, deciding on your response is not quite so clear-cut an issue. Your first response should be to turn the other cheek, to love those who trespass against you (Rule no.2). Don't be angry. Forgive the other person his misdeed. Be patient and tolerant. If a wrong has been done, perhaps it was unintentional or accidental. Talk it over. Everyone is entitled to a hearing. If someone is meeting you and he is late, for example, it would be wrong to fly off the handle the first time this happens. You might like to talk about it, but do so *calmly*. If it happens again, do the same again.

But, following Rule no.2, only let this happen twice. I don't advise giving third, fourth or fifth chances or warnings. Each time you do something good to someone who does something bad, the misdeed is strengthened. Remember Rule no. 1: rewarding behaviour reinforces it — that applies to good and bad behaviour alike.

So why give someone two chances before you consider any further action? Because it's a reasonable risk. Many people don't need tougher treatment when they act badly. All it takes for mature and untroubled people to change their behaviour is an explanation or a discussion.

But if two talks don't work, what then? Some people insist that we should always return good behaviour for bad behaviour. Not twice, but every time. They feel that the Bible's message that we should forgive those who trespass against us means we should tolerate endless bad behaviour in the belief that the wrongdoer will eventually change.

I don't accept this. It doesn't make sense to reward and strengthen bad behaviour by tolerating it. It's one thing to forgive a wrong (which means not getting angry) but quite another to tolerate a wrong (which means not making the perpetrator regret the act). I believe we act most ethically when we always forgive all bad behaviour but tolerate it no more than twice.

So rather than give someone a third chance, what should you do? There are four options when dealing with a situation which you find unacceptable:

Option no. 1: *Toleration without resentment.*
Option no. 2: *Protest.*
Option no. 3: *Separation.*
Option no. 4: *Toleration with resentment.*

Which one you choose will depend on how frustrated you are, how dangerous the situation is, and how long it has existed. The first three can help reduce the tension you'll be feeling, while the fourth will increase the tension and should be avoided if at all possible. One strategy is to go through the first three options in turn, reverting to the first if the third is unacceptable. Let's now study the four courses of action and note their advantages and disadvantages.

If you learn not to alarm yourself over frustrations, to keep a level head, and not get panicky or angry because you're not getting what you want, you'll be amazed at how much nonsense you'll be able to *tolerate without resentment*, to 'lump gracefully', as Dr Ellis puts it.

If you can't change the situation, it's perhaps best simply to put up with it. The beauty of this approach is that the problem ceases to be a problem the moment you decide to accept it. For example, if your partner is suing you for divorce and there's no way you can persuade her to change her mind, resign yourself to the fact of the matter. What else can you do without hurting yourself? Is it so unbearable not to get your own way (remember Irrational Idea no.4 in Chapter 4)? When you believe that injustice is horrible or disastrous rather than merely regretful or irritating, you'll react in one of four ways — depression, anger, fear or procrastination. However, if you take the attitude that life is unfair and you have to tolerate a certain measure of unfairness, and if you can do that without feeling resentment, you'll avoid emotional disturbances, remain composed and be better able to get on with your life.

We all use Option no. 1 constantly. And wisely so. If we were so foolish as to complain and get worked up over every wrong we encountered, life would be unbearable. But what if we have to complain? Suppose a young lady does not want to tolerate her fiancé's use of drugs. Or suppose a factory worker finds his work space cluttered by the previous shift, despite his having already twice asked the people on that shift to try and keep it tidy, and he no longer wants to tolerate the situation. Both the young lady and the factory worker can decide to *protest*.

The purpose of this strategy is to make the person

responsible for your frustration so uncomfortable that his objectionable behaviour lessens or stops: any pleasure or satisfaction he derives from his behaviour must be overshadowed by the pain or suffering he will endure if he doesn't change. This is a strategy workers have been using in their dealings with management for years. If the company doesn't agree to wage increases at a desired level, the union strikes, the company loses financially, and the union stands a good chance of achieving its objectives. What they're actually doing, then, is resorting to Rule no. 3.

But even protest may not have the desired effect. If, having protested without result, you decide you still cannot tolerate the situation without resentment, it may be sensible to consider distancing yourself from the unhappy relationship or ending it outright — to consider *separation*.

If you're thinking of divorce, let me recommend this only as a last resort, not as a first. A separation of three to six months is quite often successful in getting a difficult partner to appreciate all you've done and not just take everything for granted. Only recently, one of my male clients called his separated wife of two weeks and apologized sincerely for taking for granted all the things she had done for him, things he was now having to do for himself. She was delighted to hear how he was missing her: at the time of writing, however, she has not yet returned. Having left someone, don't go back until you see proof that some changes have been made. Don't listen to promises like 'Come back and I'll show you how much I can change'. Offer the counterargument 'I'll come back but only if you show me some changes first'. Then, if your religion allows divorce, you can resort to that if things don't change. If that's not a feasible option, you can stay separated until your partner shapes up.

There you have three rational choices when confronting a source of frustration: accept it, try and change it, or walk away from it. Each method has the potential to relieve the problem. This relief is instant if you tolerate the problem without resentment. It may be hard earned if you decide to protest. If you walk away, you at least give yourself the chance to resume your life elsewhere or with others and find peace.

Option no. 4, *toleration with resentment*, is the choice I do not recommend as it will only increase your misery. Unfortunately, it does seem to be the most popular of all the options we've considered. This is what I call the 'neurotic solution' to the problem: you won't protest, you won't walk away from the problem, so you do the worst thing possible — you accept it and resent doing so. This will only make you depressed, angry, maybe even affect your health. Far better to resort to one of the other three options. That's easy for me to say, I know, and far harder for you to do, but if you can learn not to get disturbed by the bad things that other people do to you, you can eliminate Option no. 4. Study Chapter 4 on controlling your emotions, work hard at it, and you'll be well on the way to never again having to tolerate anything without resentment.

While we're on the subject of emotions, you will recall from the description of Rule no.3 that four emotions must be avoided if this course of action is to be used effectively: anger, guilt, pity, and fear of rejection or injury. Unless you conquer these conditions it will be a miracle if you manage to gain control of your life. These emotions are well capable of defeating 99 per cent of any otherwise effective action.

When you stand up for your rights with *anger*, you're being aggressive. Do so without anger and you're being *assertive*. This has much more going for it. If you stand up to someone who has hurt you, you can count on running into resistance. Pressuring him to change could conceivably make him even nastier. So you can imagine how much you're going to achieve if you fuel the situation with anger of your own. Be firm and calm, however, and you stand a far higher chance of success. Don't give the other person further reason to fight you. The nicer you are, even if you're being uncooperative, the nicer he is going to be to you. If you can calm him down, you're far more likely to settle the problem once and for all.

This is an appropriate moment to remind you never to forget Rule no. 1. This can only help you avoid anger. Let's consider an example. A woman whose husband is lazy finally protests by refusing to cook. Calmly she tells him that she can understand that he often doesn't feel like mowing the lawn or taking the dog for a walk. He must therefore understand if she doesn't feel like cooking. She invites him out to supper. On the way out to the car he opens the kitchen door. She thanks him.

Can you see that she's using two rules at once? She's responding to his laziness with some laziness of her own (Rule no. 3). At the same time she's responding to an act of kindness with a kindness of her own (Rule no. 1). This can only help her achieve the change in behaviour she wants. What would she achieve by saying 'Don't bother. I can open the stupid door myself'? That's being aggressive (the anger, remember?) rather than assertive. You can get more flies with honey than with vinegar. So go ahead and frustrate those who frustrate you, but do it *nicely*, rewarding them for any nice things they do as they learn to behave as you want them to.

If you feel *guilt* because of something you've done in an effort to stand up to someone who is frustrating you, you'll cave in like a house of cards. Guilt is self-hate, and the result of frequent self-criticism. Being tough on people you care for is never easy, but if you feel bad about yourself it's quite simply impossible. Learn never to hate yourself, even when you've behaved wrongly. Hate your unworthy actions, to be sure. But never hate yourself, because only then can you stand up with strength to any wrong you feel worthy of correction. If you care enough about others to endure their distress when you penalize them for their sake, you're showing a rare form of love. But if you *must* hate yourself, then do it only when you have tolerated bad behaviour.

How can you possibly stand up for yourself or train others

to behave maturely if you give in to *pity* the moment you make them feel uncomfortable about their actions? To bring about change in someone's behaviour you must make the consequences of that behaviour more painful than any pleasure it gives that person, so that they'll think twice before they act so selfishly. Back down because you feel pity and you'll never achieve what you've set out to do.

Fear of rejection and making mistakes are the two most common fears people have, rejection being probably the most common of all. That's why people panic when others get angry, and avoid standing up to others' bad behaviour. But rejection is not painful unless we make it so. It is merely uncomfortable. Granted, no one in his right mind wants to be thought badly of. But being disliked or rejected is hardly the end of the world. It's happened to all of us and we've all survived it. The secret here is in how you choose to deal with it — whether or not you *choose* to upset yourself.

When you are able to control anger, guilt, pity and fear of rejection or harm there is practically nothing left that can change your mind once you have decided on a particular course of action. Backing up your words with actions is tough, certainly. But it becomes a great deal easier if you can keep control of those self-defeating emotions. Go back to Chapter 4 on controlling emotional disturbances, which will show you how this can be done. It's not easy, it'll take hard work and lots of practice, but you can do it.

Putting it into practice

Here are some examples of when and how to use Rule no. 3 for maximum effect, to give you a better idea of how the technique works. Many of the people I've helped started out unconvinced, and you may be asking yourself the same questions, but when they tried it they found it was true that you get respect when you have the power and the willingness to use your power to make others uncomfortable.

*   *   *

Tom's wife had the irritating habit of being tardy. He spoke to her often about how he liked being on time, that he felt pressed when driving to a social event, and sometimes drove recklessly to make up for lost time. Since he had been tolerant of this behaviour at least twice (more like two dozen times) I suggested it was time to look at the choices open to him: he could decide to accept that as one of her shortcomings (Option no.1), get her to change by protesting (Option no. 2), leave her (Option no. 3), or get emotionally upset (Option no. 4 — *Toleration with Resentment*). He decided to protest.

'Then let me tell you how to do that, Tom', I said. 'Do something similar, or identical to her behaviour and do it without anger, guilt, pity, or fear of rejection.'

He asked what I could suggest. 'Keep her waiting the next time she needs to be somewhere on time.'

Tom laughed and then raised the usual objections most clients give me: he didn't want to play games; he didn't want revenge; two wrongs don't make a right; and he didn't want to lower himself to her level. Let's look at these objections more closely and I'll show you that they are not valid.

First, playing games. There is nothing trivial about this strategy. It is highly recommended so that something efficient can be done about a behaviour that is slowly eating away at the good will existing between two parties.

Second, revenge. Rule no. 3 does not involve an act of revenge, rather an act of correction. Tom wants to teach his wife a simple lesson in social etiquette. And he wants to be treated with respect and consideration. He did not marry her so he could be kept waiting for no good reason. He is being a loving husband and is helping her grow. He doesn't want to hurt her, merely make her sufficiently uncomfortable until she respects his needs to a reasonable degree.

Had he made a date and kept her waiting an hour and done so *with* anger, then that would have been revenge. And that does not induce co-operation and respect, only fear and hatred. That's how wars begin, whether they be between parents and children or between mighty nations.

Let me show you further how you have often discouraged bad behaviour with unpleasant behaviour of your own. When your child scribbles on your wall, do you tolerate it? If so, you encourage it. Instead, you immediately and automatically resort to Rule no. 3 and make the child clean the wall, or send the child to its bedroom. Are you being vengeful or instructive? Do you hate your child or do you still love him and want to help him act responsibly? That's tough love, not revenge. And that's being self-interested, not self-negligent. When parents raise children they can be proud of, they have performed an important service for themselves and for the children.

Third, two wrongs don't make a right. Well of course they don't. But where *is* the wrong? Are we not being intolerant of thoughtless behaviour? Are we not interested in helping people act maturely? It is not the act which is wrong, it is the *intention* of the act which is wrong. We are trying to be helpful in the long run, and we are willing to sacrifice short-term rejection to achieve it. Tom will no doubt be under fire from his wife as he tries to modify her tardiness. That's the price he must pay to make her change. So be it. If he succeeds, they both win (provided she wants compatibility with him).

Finally, lowering yourself. Of course you don't want to stoop to the immature and unfair tactics of the person frustrating you. But what option do you have? You've tried reasoning already, haven't you? You've exhausted Rule no.2. That being the case you're left with little choice but to stop communicating with *words* and communicate with *actions* instead. When those actions are similar to those of the person who frustrates you, he or she will almost certainly get your message because you are then speaking a language that person understands.

*　　　*　　　*

'Dr Hauck, do I have the right to disagree with my mother?' asked a young woman in her thirties. 'She makes me feel guilty if I think for myself. She reminds me to respect and honour her and tells me all the time I'm not showing her love if I think for myself. Do I have the right?'

I answered, 'Do you want some coffee?'

'No', she replied with some hesitation.

'How do you know?'

'How do I know what?'

'That you don't want coffee?'

'I just don't. What do you want me to say?'

'Look, you don't want some coffee because your body is telling you so. How do you know when you're tired and want to go to bed? Or when to get up? Or when you want to express your thoughts? Or when you feel frustrated or you don't feel frustrated? If the frustration is minor, you probably ignore it. If it's strong, you do something about it. And you feel that need to do something throughout your whole body. You ask me if you should talk up to people you disagree with. Isn't it a big frustration?'

'Yes it is.'

'Can you tolerate it without resentment?'

'No.'

'Then either train your mother not to put you down when you express yourself, or have little to do with her.'

(Do you recognize Options no. 2 and no. 3?)

I went on to explain to my client that when we are under stress and feel unsatisfied and uncomfortable with our lives, it is imperative to do something to change our frustrations or shut up. I can't tell someone to stand up to her mother because I don't know how much the problem troubles her, but she does.

If she doesn't want to put up with the problem or to walk away from it, then she has the choice, no, she has the moral obligation, to protest and put an end to the evil.

How do you decide when to make waves? Doesn't that depend on many considerations? Yes and no. When you think over what the consequences will be if you disagree with your mother, or tell off your boss, or send back a chair your spouse purchased without consulting you first, you'll be able to decide if you'd be reasonably comfortable if you ignored the whole matter. If so, ignore it. If not, protest, for you would then not be *just reasonably content* (JRC). And that is serious.

The point where you feel so dissatisfied that you are not even reasonably or barely content is the time you had better raise your level of contentment. It doesn't normally matter the reason someone frustrates you, if you are very unhappy, talk yourself out of being disturbed or stand up to your spouse, child, or parent until you do feel reasonably content. Mind you, that's nothing to feel guilty about because you'd only be *barely* content if you got your way. For the moment that may be enough. At least you can say that the marriage isn't half bad even though you ideally would want things going your way much more. As long as you're just reasonably content you're looking out for your basic interests without hopefully putting others out so much that they too become less than reasonably satisfied. If that happens it may mean you two are not compatible and that a separation is called for.

Do you have the right to protest? The answer to this is fairly straightforward. If you don't, three consequences will occur that will hurt you and anyone you're dealing with. First, you'll become *unhappy* at the very least and quite likely also *disturbed*. Living below the JRC is like living on less food each day than it takes to maintain your health. I have counselled literally thousands of people who existed on less than reasonable contentment, not for hours or days, or weeks, but for months and years, as much as ten, twenty, thirty years! Can you imagine such self-neglect? Furthermore, can you imagine how little happiness these people were able to give their families, or their employers? If they weren't depressed and fatigued a good deal of the time, then they were at least ill with headaches or insomnia, weepy, and passive. The family senses their insecurity and takes shameful advantage of my clients once they're down on one knee, ready for the knockout.

These unhappy men and women set poor examples for their children and for each other. They give quiet permission to those around them to be rude, selfish, inconsiderate, and perhaps physically abusive, all in the hope that by being tolerant again and again, the thoughtless people would feel so loved that they would eventually change. How sad, and how naïve.

Second, you will eventually *fall out of love*. That's the next consequence for living chronically below the JRC. It makes no difference how determined you were to make your relationship succeed. If your deepest desires and needs are not met to a reasonable degree you will fall out of love as surely as you will lose weight if you don't eat. Love simply lives on what your lover does for you — no satisfactions, no love — unless you're a saint or a martyr. Everybody else falls out of love.

Third, you *break away*. You quit the job, move to a new neighbourhood, find another friend, order your grown children out of the home, or leave your partner. You may not believe in a separation or a divorce but after you've been miserable for months or years you may consider these solutions with open arms.

If you don't want to become disturbed, turn against your loved ones, or leave them, don't put others' interests before your own as long as your body tells you you're not just reasonably content. Until you regain contentment, do anything within decency and fairness to raise your sense of well-being until you are not unhappy or disturbed, you are not falling out of love, and you don't want to break off the relationship.

*　　　*　　　*

Now let's assume you have determined to protest against your neighbour's loud parties and have called the police. You did it without anger, guilt, pity, or fear of rejection or harm. The police break up the party and everyone goes home. Beautiful, right? Wrong. You did a bad thing to your neighbour and he's displeased and wants to teach you not to spoil *his* fun. Count on his wanting to train you never to call the police on him again. He can use Rule no. 3 just as readily as you can. He may not know how to use it without getting angry and that's why he'll be scary to deal with. Therefore, expect him to threaten you physically, to ignore you, to turn the neighbourhood against you, and so on.

So what are you to do in return? Follow Rule no. 3 again. If he offends you, politely bother him again. If he throws another loud party take him to court. If he threatens you physically, sue. In short, whenever people get nasty with you for trying to train them to treat you decently, get tougher and tougher with them until they stop being thoughtless.

If they get too nasty and you can't change them, then consider them untrainable and accept Option no. 1 (Toleration without Resentment), or Option no. 3 (Separation). But if you want to protest until one of you gets reasonable satisfaction, who usually wins the power struggle? The answer will surprise you. In any struggle, the one who wins is the one who cares the *least* for the relationship. For example, you and your child may counterattack many times as you each try to train the other. As one penalty doesn't work, the next will be sterner. No matter how nasty you each get, the struggle will reach a point where it is so intolerable that one of you will give in, or one of you will break away. And it is the one who cares the *least* for the relationship who will win.

The teenager who doesn't care if he loses his car will defy his parents until they sell it. The worker who hates his job and can find another will tell his boss to do the dirty work himself, and will not fear being fired. The partner who cares the least about the marriage is the one who will get his or her way about moving the family to a new city. If the threat of a separation or divorce has no impact on one member of a couple, then that one will hold out longest in the power struggle.

This is clearly unfair, I agree. But that's the way it works.

*   *   *

'What do you do to a son who steals money from you?' a tearful mother asked me. The fifteen-year-old adolescent stole from his mother's purse and splurged on his buddies in order to play the big shot.

I first advised that she not get angry, just firm. I went into the dynamics of anger and depression so that she could deal with her son and his problems. Then we got to the matter of assertion.

The boy had possessions (a radio, record player, and sports equipment) which had value. I suggested she take whatever of his she needed until the value of those items equalled the amount he stole (I believe it was about $50). She could sell those items and give him the balance beyond what he stole, or she could donate them to charity.

The youngster was furious, of course, but his mother did it without explanation. While he was at school she took what she needed, and dealt with him that night. She told him quietly why she took his things and was pleasant throughout. That made it harder for the boy to influence her behaviour and it convinced him she meant business. Have you ever noticed how much more you believe someone when a statement is made quietly rather than by screaming at the top of your voice?

The mother didn't succeed the first time she did this to her son. But when she did it twice more when he stole from her, he finally got the message and kept his hands off her things.

Another good way to deal with uncooperative children

occurred to me when I was giving therapy to one young fellow. His father drove fifty miles with him to keep their appointment. The father took time off work and wanted me to teach his son better study habits. Well, wouldn't you know it, after I talked to the father for thirty minutes to get the facts, I excused him and called in the boy. He wasn't exactly co-operative. In fact he was rude and told me he didn't want to talk to me, wasn't going to, and didn't give a damn.

I attempted to get on his good side, to make him less defensive, so I could help him get better grades. No such luck. He told me to drop dead and a few other things.

I excused him, called back his father and asked him if his son had money of his own. Well, it turned out he did. If you know what Rule no. 3 is all about, guess what I advised the father to do. You guessed it. I told the father to make the boy pay for the half hour he wasted.

When the young man got home he exploded. His father remained firm, brought him back in a week, and would you believe it — he did it again! So he was charged again.

This went on for three visits and then the boy cooled off, made good use of his sessions and gave me a chance to teach him better study habits. Thanks to a father who loved his son enough to tolerate hate and rejection, everything worked out just fine.

*   *   *

A young couple suddenly complicated their lives when the lady, a college student, became pregnant. Marriage was not possible while he was unemployed but he wanted all the privileges of visiting his son without paying for his support.

She reasoned with him repeatedly over the necessity of getting a job so they could marry. His promises to find work came to nothing and she became bitter over having all the work of caring for her infant with none of the security of a marriage.

I advised her to make him uncomfortable over his conduct or he'd not want to change. In my opinion she was helping him become the sort of man she could not love, and only by urging him to be responsible would she ever have the respect and love for him she wanted. To do that she would have to protest against his laziness to such a degree that he would change and assume his moral duties as the child's father.

Being nice to him hadn't worked. Reasoning hadn't budged him. He wanted something for nothing. It was time to stop tolerating his procrastination by not rewarding unacceptable behaviour. I advised her not to see him or allow him access to the baby until he had earned the right.

She refused his phone calls and declined all discussion of marriage until he had the financial means. This was not easy for her. Feeling guilty over frustrating him, and pitying him for his pain, she weakened occasionally and let him back into her life. That led to more feelings of being manipulated, again followed by firmness.

He accused her of selfishness, being hateful, and that she would cause great mental harm to their son unless she married him and let him become involved. She protested that he wasn't involved and couldn't be until he took his obligations seriously and could prove it.

He finally got the message and realized that he couldn't manipulate her. In short order he did obtain work, saved his money and became an eligible husband. She saw the change and accepted his proposal after he had supported her for several months and given every indication he would continue. I was convinced it would not have happened had she continued to tolerate his wanting to have his cake and to eat it too.

*   *   *

Every so often a client comes to me to learn to cope with a partner who is addicted to spending wildly. One fellow I recall tried to reason with his wife until he ran out of patience. Then he yelled and insisted on taking over their cheque account and cut up the credit cards. That only slowed her up for a few months. Eventually she sneaked the dresses and boxes of shoes into the attic hoping he wouldn't catch her for months, by which time he might cool off.

I suspected she resorted to this habit to show her anger for his neglecting her, and thus to force him to pay her more attention. It seemed a reasonable interpretation to her but it didn't change things. I therefore decided to teach her husband to be intolerant of her reckless spending.

I suggested he pack up her boxes of unnecessary purchases and either return them to the stores or donate them to charity. That scared him because she'd raise the roof, not talk to him for days and possibly leave.

He was quite correct — she might do just that. However, I pointed out that it was only natural to expect resistance from people when they are being pressured to change. That was not the issue. The true issue was: what would he do *when* she counterattacked?

He could either give in and let her spend excessively, or he could put more pressure on her to change. Or he could leave her. He decided to stop complaining, to preserve his marriage (if he could) by getting her to change the ways she was turning him off, and to make her uncomfortable enough to change. To this end he did donate boxes of her belongings to a church and the Salvation Army. When she bought a radio or stuffed chair he hadn't agreed to, he took it back to the store. He also refused to follow through on vacation plans because her buying expensive presents for a family gathering shortened their funds so much he would have had to take out a loan. She was furious, threatened to divorce him, rejected him with her silence and refused to cook for him or keep him company. He was in an emotional Siberia for weeks. The pressure often made him waver to the point where he almost gave in.

In the end, by making her more and more uncomfortable

each time she spent foolishly, she became so miserable and felt so helpless to stop him that she decided to stop the habit rather than leave him.

I was not surprised. What happened to this couple is the normal course of events when someone in a relationship is very unhappy and wants to correct that unfairness.

*   *   *

A tearful woman told me of the trouble she was having with her grown son. He repeatedly borrowed money from the elderly lady, promising always to repay her but never managing even to make a few token payments. She wanted me to talk to her son and show him how immature and selfish he was. The young man refused even to talk with me over the phone. That meant I'd have to work the problem out solely with the mother.

Her problem was clearly one of feeling guilt and pity, and fearing rejection. With these three handcuffs on her it was impossible to be an assertive person. The degree to which she had indulged him over the years slowly dawned on her. Rather than being a good and loving mother, as she always regarded herself, she began to realize how her love was only defined by how tolerant she could be, seldom by how firm. Not until he tried to blackmail her emotionally with tears, threats of suicide, and, this failing, harsh name-calling, did she accept the fact that he had gone too far, and that she had indulged him excessively.

She therefore wrote him a letter informing him of her regrets for not having prepared him carefully for life and that she would henceforth not support a grown man with a college education any longer. If he couldn't get along on his income he'd have to move to smaller quarters, sell his car, or get a better job. The choice was his. Furthermore, if he phoned her to try and change her mind by appealing to her guilt or sympathy, she would hang up without hesitation. And if that did not work and he still refused to grow up, she would cut him out of whatever was still left in her estate.

These were among the first and few truly loving acts she performed for her son for many years. Instead of weakening to an adult man who was fully capable of caring for himself 200 miles away in a large city with endless opportunities, she was finally discouraging dependent behaviour.

He did not commit suicide (although the possibility always existed, of course), he was sufficiently fearful of being cut out of the will, and he eventually changed his tune from one of disrespect to one of respect. She struggled with a sense of guilt and with pity for him but was firm and always polite. In time she learned that you get respect when you have power and are not afraid to make others uncomfortable with it.

*   *   *

My next example will hopefully illustrate the dangers of not being assertive by reason of some past psychological problem.

He counselled with me, his wife refused. She had fallen out of love and left him. After a time she returned, apologized and asked him to continue the marriage. This happened twice. He forgave her each time, paid her bills, and hoped for the best. She had been a rejected child, distrusted people, and could not allow herself to become intimate for any length of time.

My analysis of their troubles clearly indicated that he was rewarding her for leaving him rather than frustrating her. If he could get her to therapy to understand her need to escape, they could work things out. Good thinking — up to a point. The trouble was that she had no intention of working on her problem. His tolerating a revolving-door marriage was clearly making things worse. I suggested he not allow her to return the next time until she entered therapy or lived on her own for six months and still felt she loved him enough to stay. If so, he'd go through this one more time — no more.

She agreed. Some months later she left again. He was all set to tolerate this 'because of her childhood rejections'. I reminded him of those two principles of learning: we get the behaviour we allow; and if we want others to change, we must change first. If he didn't *do* something about her problem, she'd probably never change. By neglecting his interests almost totally he was hurting them both. In time, if he wouldn't encourage her to change he'd suffer the three consequences of living below the JRC for a long time. In fact, I already strongly suspected he was unhappy and disturbed. First his sleep was disturbed and his friends observed that he was more on edge. Second, though he found it hard to admit it, he was less in love. And third, he had fleeting thoughts of calling up his attorney and going ahead with a divorce.

After asking me one day what he should do I again told him what his options were. He could accept her behaviour and stop complaining about it. When there were no serious problems they got along quite well. Perhaps her childhood problem would weaken as she matured. He had put up with this pattern for a few years already, why couldn't he continue to do so?

Or he could pressure her to change: treat her as badly as she treated him. Maybe she'd appreciate what she was putting him through if he put her through the wringer a few times. As long as he did this to help the woman he needn't have any reason to feel guilty or to pity her. And if he could sweat out a period of rejection and anger, she might come around.

Or he could separate or divorce.

Or he could drive himself nuts by keeping his mouth shut but resenting it deeply. If he didn't mind headaches, ulcers, and feeling generally miserable, I told him, he could be my guest.

He wanted to try working on the problem one more time. So I advised him to give her three to six months and if he wasn't convinced she was making progress, to either tolerate her without resentment (Option no. 1) or leave her (Option no. 3).

Before the six months were up he could see she wasn't ready to change. He chose to leave her and did.

*   *   *

A woman who attended one of my seminars on assertion complained that her daughter repeatedly asked her to iron her dress on Sunday evening, shortly before the mother was ready to go to bed. She yelled at her daughter and told her every week how unfair such a request was, and how she wanted her to ask to have the clothes ironed on Saturday or earlier on Sunday. She said one thing but did another — another example of how we believe what others do, not what they say. The girl's mother rewarded the girl's asking to have the dress ironed on Sunday night.

I told her never to iron a dress late Sunday night and the girl would soon learn to make the request at a time more convenient to the mother. Wouldn't you know it, the mother immediately justified doing it Sunday night anyway because 'I couldn't send my daughter to school in a wrinkled dress'.

Of course she could (even though it would reflect upon her as a good mother). So I reminded the mother not to complain if the problem wasn't important enough to weather a little criticism from the teachers or the neighbours.

That did it and she told me some weeks later the girl was properly retrained after the mother let her daughter suffer some embarrassment for two or three weeks by going to school in unironed clothes. Case closed!

*   *   *

Every example above is about one or more persons who suffered from serious self-neglect. They wanted to get along with someone who frustrated them but were not allowed to. Only when they stood up for their rights without anger, guilt, pity, fear of rejection, or fear of injury, and took control of their lives and taught the wrongdoer a lesson in fairness, did these victims become self-interested persons to a reasonable degree.

6

Friendship and Social Skills

Unless you enjoy being a hermit it is imperative that you learn to enjoy people. Friendships are vital for the breath of fresh air they bring into all our lives. As a clinical psychologist I have seen a great many marriages get into a rut because the partners only ever kept their own company, seldom experienced the delight of sharing a meal with other couples, and could never trust each other to be alone with others. If you're going to make and keep friends, there are three psychological problems which you must overcome: shyness, aggression and self-centredness.

Shyness

Shy people are afraid of being laughed at, being thought poorly of, being put down and made to feel inferior, and finally, of being rejected. They are so convinced of their unworthiness that they are certain everyone else will be as convinced of that fact as they are. When they meet people they automatically view others as superior, threatening, and ready to reject them. Though they may have many opportunities to meet people, to start conversations, to break into small groups at a party and introduce themselves, they will seldom do this, for fear of rejection.

The more they do this the more afraid they become. Then, when meeting others, they will turn their eyes away. Or they will blush. Or they will shake hands in a weak and limp manner. These are signals to the other person that here is a shy, scared, and inferior-feeling person. They could just as well wear a T-shirt bearing the message: 'I am not as good as you are. I know you're not going to like me.'

To overcome shyness it is imperative that you question the idea that you are somehow totally inferior to practically everyone you talk to. You are not. Think of it this way: we are all inferior to other people in certain respects. The person you want to talk to may be a better wage earner, a better singer, have more education, and so on. But you undoubtedly have some talents which the person you're addressing does not have or has in lesser measure. Perhaps you can garden, cook, take good photographs, tear an engine apart, or play a banjo. Most of us have something we can do better than someone else. But the shy person does not see this. He concludes that, because he is inferior in one or more ways, he is *totally* inferior and must feel ashamed.

Learn to make sensible comparisons. You will not frequently be rejected because you lack certain characteristics. Some people may not like you on the first meeting because of your dialect, skin colour, or appearance. You probably judge others in the same way. Ask yourself if the people you feel superior to are totally worthless. When I ask this question of my clients they always reassure me that others are not worthless if they happen to be inferior in some ways. Then why should my clients be totally worthless when they too are inferior in some ways to millions of others?

To remedy this situation it is important that you begin to do the thing that you fear the most. Talk to people. Introduce yourself. Start a conversation, no matter where you happen to be. Start with those people who frighten you the least. Perhaps you ought to start talking to children or to old people of whom you are not afraid. When you know how to start conversations with them move up or down the age scale gradually until you are able to talk to the group you fear the most.

If you are afraid of talking to popular people then start by talking to the unpopular ones. Talk to those who are also shy. Or talk to those who are not particularly good looking, or who have very little power or social prestige. In this way you will start at a point where you are not very threatened, and where you can begin to face your fear ever so slightly. You cannot start far enough away to make a beginning. That is a cardinal principle to observe. No matter what you fear, you can usually get far enough away from it so that you can work up to it gradually.

From there you cannot make the steps forward too small. No matter how slightly you decrease your distance from the thing that you fear, it is always better than nothing. Any progress, however slow, is still progress. People seem to give up too quickly in the belief that they are not making progress, when in fact they are. Their mistake is that they compare their actual progress with their expectations. A man who thinks a little therapy is going to bring him out of his shell and get him married to the belle of the ball will be mightily disappointed when six months later he concludes that he is only now getting to the point where he can phone one of his female co-workers. He certainly cannot boast of great progress when he considers how far he still has to go. But from my point of view he is improving and he ought to be pleased with his progress. If he is dating two or three women in the next half year and manages to get married in the next year or two, how can he complain? 'What,' you ask, 'spend two years just trying to make contact with a woman and maybe eventually getting married?' Yes. You had better understand that social skills are every bit as complicated as are other skills which take a long time to learn.

The pain of socializing

Every shy person cries away from going to parties or asking others if they may join them because of the considerable discomfort they know they'll experience if they do the social thing. Some sweat under the arms, others tremble at the knees, and still others get so tense they stammer, look away, or blush. Any of these symptoms are easily understood as signs of distress. And that's precisely what the shy person does not want to be common knowledge — that he or she is socially petrified.

Granted, the first moments after the introduction and during the following conversation can be quite unnerving. They don't have to be, of course, and they also don't always last very long once a conversation gets going. To the shy person, nevertheless, it is a time of slow death. They are worried about having something to say, whether they'll say something dumb and make fools of themselves, or if their nervousness will be so obvious others will spot it in an instant.

All these considerations are irrelevant — totally irrelevant. Sweat blood if you must. Stammer if you must. Whatever you do, don't avoid the encounter.

If you tell yourself very quickly that this discomfort is not going to kill you, that these people are not going to reject you, that even if they did, it wouldn't be the end of the world, and that these people are no different from you except in some very specific ways (as they, too, differ from all the other people at the party), you'll face the music and smile and talk.

The more often you do this the easier it will get and the day will surely come when you'll be less fearful and socialize better. Then you'll be glad you put up with the discomfort at the beginning and faced a difficult task instead of avoiding it. However, if you don't face the task for the sake of an immediate relief, it will simply get harder and harder.

In short, no matter what you do; give the speech, host the party, or call someone for a date. If you don't, you will be uncomfortable. To do or not to do then rests on only one consideration: which choice results in the *least* pain. The answer? Facing a difficult task is overwhelmingly easier in the long run. Granted, if you have reason to believe you'll die in a month, forget what I just said. Eat, drink and be merry, for you are not long for this world. Why discipline yourself when there is no tomorrow to reap the reward? However, if you're likely to live a long time then face your problems now or you'll have the problem hanging around your neck for the rest of your life. I know, I've seen otherwise bright and mature people in their fifties and sixties just as shy as a fifteen-year-old child.

We have all known of brave people who climb mountains, dive out of aeroplanes, earn medals for heroism, but who are ridiculously shy. This means that they are less afraid of things that can kill them than they are of things that can't. That doesn't make much sense, does it? Shy people frequently fly in aeroplanes which can crash. But they are not afraid to fly. They take elevators that can drop. But they are not afraid to use them.

And we all drive around in cars that kill over 50,000 people in the United States each year and cripple about a million. Yet none of us quiver, sweat, or shake whenever we step into our cars. We look forward to it. We enjoy the scenery and listen to music while rolling along at high speeds, relatively unmindful of the fact that a tyre could blow or that a drunk could be coming from an opposite direction. We know that could happen but that doesn't stop us from driving. Yet all these things I have mentioned are positively dangerous and often fatal when something goes wrong.

Now compare those situations with being introduced to a few strangers at a cocktail party. There is not a ghost of a chance that any of those people are going to pull out a machine gun and shoot you. None of them is going to gang up on you and beat you to a pulp. They are not going to grab you and throw you out of the window. They are all going to size you up a bit just as you are sizing them up to see if there is anything that you have in common with them or they with you. Then they will move on and chat with someone else. That is not dangerous. That can never be fatal. It is a totally harmless experience, yet it is perceived by millions of people around the world as positively frightening and even terrifying.

'I don't know what to talk about'

One of the most ridiculous things that I keep hearing shy people say is that they don't want to make light conversation because they don't know what to say. They seem to think there are some mysterious things that everyone else seems to know how to talk about but not they. Or they believe they have to be informed on a particular subject that happens to be up for discussion at the moment or they can't participate in that conversation.

Let me suggest that when you are engaged in a conversation and you're not sure what the other person would be interested in, just talk about anything. If the conversation rolls along nicely, you'll hit on a good subject. If it doesn't, in all likelihood your listener will respond and perhaps bring up a new topic. But whatever you do, just don't stand there as though you have been hit on the head with a sledgehammer not knowing what to say. Make any casual comment, it hardly has to be a brilliant one. Get the ball rolling and even start a new conversation just like you would pick up an item of food at the salad bar and then pick up another entirely different from that. You could always mention the weather, as corny as that may be, or the stock market, or what happened to your favourite sports idol. Ask questions about the other person, what he or she does, what that person enjoys eating, where he or she has travelled, if married, how many children he or she has, and so forth. Those items practically always get a conversation started.

And when you get nervous, don't just walk away just because you're sweating a bit. Be uncomfortable for a bit. If you get past that initially uncomfortable stage you can easily get to the point where the conversation begins to take off on its own, where the two of you can find something in common to talk about, and where you then might truly enjoy each other. But you're not going to do this if you immediately run off and avoid the company because you will temporarily be frustrated and upset. If you want to change, you're going to have to endure that momentary discomfort and plough ahead until your persistence pays off.

Embarrassment, humiliation and insults

Shy people are forever justifying staying away from others in the honest belief that they want to avoid embarrassment, humiliation, or insults. If they were correct about humiliations, embarrassments, or insults literally being painful, I would be the first to advise them not to get too close to others. Obviously the safest course of action, and the sanest too, would be simply to avoid close contact with people because they can hurt when they say mean things, or when they laugh at you. But I don't advise anything of the sort. I don't believe anyone can humiliate you. Nothing is embarrassing. No one can insult you.

You can humiliate yourself. *You* can turn any event into an embarrassing one. And *you* can turn any comment into an insult if you're sensitive enough. But that's *your* problem, not others'. Staying away from others doesn't cure that problem at all. Only by working it through rationally and convincing yourself that humiliation is not possible (unless you choose to be humiliated) will you cure the problem. You can't get embarrassed by anything unless you feel you had to be perfect enough to avoid a foolish act. And you can't be insulted ever if you'd examine the statement very objectively.

Let me show you how this works. Suppose you're at a party and you're telling a joke but you forget the punchline. Other people laugh and you feel humiliated. What you're actually saying is that what you did was unforgiveable. You did something so disgusting, so infantile, so totally out of keeping with your maturity, your age, and your intelligence, that it is unthinkable that you should have done it. That's why you feel embarrassed. You think you have let yourself down so completely that there is nothing else to do but crawl into a hole and close the trap door behind you.

But why shouldn't you forget a punch line? People do it all the time. It's only a mild slip of your memory and as such, it's certainly harmless enough. But the way you're taking it you'd think you had spilled soup on the president of the company, or tripped someone so he went sprawling across the floor. And come to think of it, even if you had done those things, I still don't think you'd need to be embarrassed. Again, you'd be saying that these things are unbelievably terrible, thoroughly disgusting, and unthinkable for a person with your intelligence and sophistication. But why are they? Whoever said they were? Why can't you have an accident while you're entertaining the president of your company in your home, or why can't you forget someone's name whom you've known for quite sometime and you're not able to introduce that person to someone else? Why is that so horrendous?

Embarrassment is merely a very harsh judgement against yourself. I and other RET therapists staunchly maintain that you need never judge yourself for anything. Judge your behaviour, correct it if you can, and learn by your mistakes, certainly. But convincing yourself that you're no good, worthless, totally undesirable, or evil, and that you ought to be ashamed of yourself is utter nonsense. All that you've proved by any of these acts, and those which are even a great deal worse than those, is that you're simply a human being. You have every right as a human being to do all kinds of dumb things which I hope you will try very hard to change. But I hope you will also forgive yourself when you commit them. That's how you get over the embarrassment. Forgive yourself. Remind yourself that you're just imperfect, that you can try very hard but you can never avoid mistakes, bad judgements, or loss of emotional control sometimes. That's what it means to be a human being. The embarrassed person, however, says 'I demand more of myself . . . I thought I had all these things totally under control and now I discovered just this instant when I poured coffee in someone's lap that I wasn't so great after all'. So what else is new?

The fear of being insulted is also one of the powerful reasons given by shy people to justify avoiding others. This, too, is a needless concern. People cannot insult you unless you allow them to. If what they are saying is true, appreciate their comments, thank them for telling you that you're drinking too much, or that your language is offensive, and then change. Why should that be an insult? You're not perfect, you didn't realize that people were being offended by your comments, and even if you did, now they're telling you that it is offensive and if you care for the friendship, you had better just simply stop behaving in such a manner.

But if you decide their comments are wrong, and that your statements are really justified, wise, and not offensive, then obviously you must think that the people who are taking offence at your remarks are simply wrong. It is their opinion against yours. I can assure you that you will be far less intimidated when talking to others if you work through understanding how embarrassment, humiliation, and insults are harmless and can never upset you unless you permit them to do so.

Aggression

The second reason why people do not get along socially is the undercurrent of resentment, bitterness, and submerged hostility which often comes out in one's language and defensive attitudes. Take this as a standard rule: if you are angry it will eventually show through in some of your behaviour, and it will turn people away.

Life is absolutely packed with frustrations and the natural reaction to frustrations is aggression. As normal as this feeling may be, however, you must learn to control it and not be normal. Be healthy instead.

It doesn't take a genius to know that letting loose a barrage of ugly feelings is certainly not going to make us well liked. We may become notorious, but that is not the way we want to be known. When we are talking about developing positive social skills we are talking about becoming popular in a positive way, being liked by people, not feared. It is alright to be a little bit feared by people because that's how we get respect. Leaving this case aside (that a little force and firmness may sometimes be necessary to prevent being taken advantage of), the rule still holds that if you want friends, you must be nice to them. And being mean and difficult, pushing people around, yelling at them, or striking them is no way to get their respect. You'll get their fear, not their respect or love.

It is the other kinds of aggression which I want to pay more attention to. This is not the aggression of violent behaviour, it is the aggression that comes through sarcasm, malevolent teasing, constant fault-finding, making comparisons between your partner and your former lover, or your child and his or her friends, and so on. Belittling someone's efforts, even though you may do it with a smile, is aggression. Not focusing on the good the person has done, but focusing mainly on the unsatisfactory behaviour, is aggression. That's like taking a psychological punch in the nose.

It is also aggression when you want to complain about something but don't, and later, when you are unhappy because you gave in against your better judgement, you blame others because of your unhappiness. Take the case of the wife who doesn't want to go to the company picnic but goes anyway to please her husband and then doesn't have a good time. She comes home moaning about what a rotten time she had and how she doesn't like his friends. That's not fair and that's aggression.

To go to a party with an escort and then leave her seated while you chat with your friends, without introducing her – that's aggression. In other words, being inconsiderate, lacking tact, finding fault, failing to give praise where it is obviously due are all forms of psychological aggression. These acts are meant to hurt, to subdue, to conquer, not to befriend, instruct, or to help. No matter how well disguised, the person receiving such treatment feels the true intent of your behaviour automatically. You may get by with it a few times, but if you keep it up, the individual being attacked will certainly know it and the nature of that relationship will change for the worse. You may never see it (at least not openly), but if you keep it up, the child, spouse, or friend will change eventually and you will reap the sad results of that change. Your friend will leave you for someone who is more considerate than you. Children so treated develop resistance, get into power struggles, and become very oppositional. Your spouse will soon show the usual symptoms of depression, counter-aggression, or loss of affection.

Self-centredness

Putting yourself before others the vast majority of the time is going to make you greatly disliked and isolated. The only friends you will have around you are those you can buy or dominate. You may not notice that there is anything wrong in your life while you have wealth or power, but I can assure you, the moment you lose either, you'll be surprised at how quickly these people will leave you when they don't have to take any nonsense from you. And why should they?

Any fair relationship is always a balance between you getting reasonable contentment and others getting reasonable contentment. If you are constantly pushing for your own desires and ignoring those of others you will, in effect, behave like a spoiled brat. It doesn't matter how many times you get your way by arguing, pushing, or trying to make others feel guilty, you're going to create the same impression upon others as the aggressive person does. You'll get your way, and you will be happy about it. But don't forget, you are creating greater and greater frustrations in the other person who is slowly building up a dislike for you. The day may soon come when he or she won't want anything to do with you.

Stop being a prima donna. Stop thinking you always have to have the floor and say what you want without giving the other person a fair chance to speak also. Don't be greedy and always go where you want to go or do what you want to do.

That's being self-centred. The first chance your friends or family have to get away from you and do their own thing, they will. Some marriages which have lasted thirty years may end abruptly because one of the parties gets sick and tired of having to give in all the time just to keep the mate from bellyaching.

Stop thinking you're God's gift to the world and that your desires are always more important than someone else's. What you're showing others is that you're an emotional baby who can't stand being frustrated and that you can't make any compromises. I believe it was Confucius who said something to the effect that reciprocity is the basic law of human nature. This means that if I scratch your back I expect you to scratch my back. This also means that if I give in to you today I expect you to give in to me tomorrow. No matter how right you may think you are, I probably think I am just as right as you do. It is important that we get over the idea that because we think we are right we must have our way. That's simply taking a grandiose attitude about life which says that you know everything better than everyone else. And even if it were true, if you haven't convinced the other party, then you're simply going to make an enemy out of that person who truly doesn't agree with you.

It is much better in the long run to give in to others a fair share of the time. Stop being so egocentric, so spoiled and so intolerant of having to put up with a frustration. When you look around, you'll be amazed at how many people have never really grown up. They can still be emotional children between the ages of twenty and seventy. Some grandmothers and grandfathers still rule their children with their own infantile demands for self-satisfaction. What surprises me is how often these people feel indignant that people don't want to talk to them, phone them, include them in parties, or visit them. In truth, why should they be catered to? What they often end up being is royal pains in the neck. Yet, so filled with grandiosity are these poor souls who think that they must have everything they want they can't even see what they are doing to their friends and families when it is apparent to everybody that they are extremely selfish people who don't give a hoot about others.

Therefore, if you find yourself alienated and cut out of social contacts, don't blame others, ask yourself why people are finding you do undesirable. Be ruthless about this self-analysis and if you fit the description I have just given, then be a more kindly person, do more for others, do more to be liked, and stop insisting that you must have everything you want. Mature people in particular won't stand the likes of you. Yet they will be the ones whose friendship you will probably want to cultivate the most, while you will be the kind of person they will want to avoid the most.

Summary

Developing sound social skills is one of those activities which brings us enormous rewards. If you do not cultivate this skill you will find yourself left out of most of the fun times adults can have. Eating alone, being excluded from social occasions, going on trips alone, are all part of the consequences which people with poor social skills suffer. To avoid this consequence I urge you first to try to overcome your fear of people; second, to try to overcome your anger when you're frustrated and deal with people assertively instead of aggressively; and lastly, to stop being self-centred.

7

Health and Wealth

Health

To get the most out of life you need not only a healthy mind, one that is well trained to perform skilled tasks and that knows how to talk the body out of getting very upset, but also a healthy body. If you smoke for a lifetime and have ruined your lungs, the quality of your life goes down in direct proportion to your inability to take a deep breath. If you are overweight and can't play tennis, hike, or even take normal walks, your lifestyle deteriorates. If you overdrink and ruin your liver, you can die. If you eat too many sweets or eat too much fat, research indicates that you might have a heart attack long before others your age.

In short, among the most important factors which determine the kind of life you have is the kind of health you have. This is such an obvious statement that it's often not considered seriously. We take our health for granted — until we lose it. Anytime you want to find out what your life would be like if you were paralysed, just put yourself in a wheelchair and don't use your legs for three days. And if you want to find out what it is like not to see, wear a blindfold for a day and see what life can be like.

I think you get the point. Staying healthy is as essential for the body as tuning an engine is for a car. The shame of this whole business is the fact that we know more about cars than we know about our bodies. But it does appear fortunately, that Western society is finally changing and becoming much more health-conscious. More people are following diet and exercise programmes than ever before. Wherever we look we see articles in the newspapers, magazines and discussions on radio and television about diet and exercise that tell us how to live longer and happier lives. Many of you who are reading this book who are not up on some of the major findings on health today are very likely to have a shorter and less healthy life.

What can be accomplished

To help convince you that living with proper exercise and diet has enormous benefit let me point to some findings that have come out of the Longevity Center in Santa Barbara, California. These people advise caution in diet, they advise cutting back on the five primary foods which they feel will cause a deterioration of health: sugar, salt, caffeine, cholesterol and fat. They also advise exercising by jogging or walking at least every other day. It is the contention of the staff of the Longevity Center that anyone following this regime can live to be 90 or more, the age he or she would be expected to live to if born in the year 2000.

Some of the people who frequent the Center are in their eighties and nineties and are amazingly physically active. Many of them run miles every day, have stable blood pressure and heart rhythms and seem, according to the director of the Center, Nathan Pritikin, to be an unusually healthy group of people.

But Pritikin has excited a certain amount of controversy and certainly not all of the authorities on health will agree with his findings. However, all the research I have come across from university groups or other private research groups points more or less in the same direction. Practically every one of these authorities encourages us to reduce fats, salt, and cholesterol and to exercise a moderate amount — about thirty minutes three or more days a week. On this there is practically no dispute. And people who follow this regime are beginning to show clear superiority over others who do not follow it.

How to increase your life span

Statistics tell us that men will live to be around 70 and women to be about 76. Obviously some will die before that time and others will live beyond that life expectancy. The question arises whether or not it is possible to influence a person's life span since it is generally thought that one's genes or particular biological make-up are the determining factors in how long a person lives.

A study by Dr Ralph S. Paffenbarger, Jr, and his associates from Stanford University, California, indicates that exercise can in fact have a very definite effect on how long a person lives. He and his colleagues studied 16,939 Harvard graduates who entered college between 1916 and 1950 and whose ages ranged from 35 to 74 when the study began. The subjects were followed from the 1960s until 1978. They were given exercises which included such activities as walking, climbing stairs, and engaging in different sports.

The findings were published in the *New England Journal of Medicine*, where it was stated that 'mortality rates were significantly lower among the physically active'. But, more than this, it seems that a regular exercise programme had the effect of counteracting the negative effects of hypertension, cigarette smoking, and weight problems, as well as the 'genetic tendency to die young'. They found that those men who were hypertensive and exercised could reduce 'their risk of dying by more than half, while hypertensives who did not exercise moved into the highest risk category'.

Those individuals who walked nine or ten miles a week had a 21% lower mortality rate than those who only walked three miles or less. And those who were in sports for one or two hours a week increased their life expectancy by 24% over those who did not.

Those of you who do not exercise regularly are making life comfortable for yourself for the moment, but don't think you're doing yourself a great favour. Remember our discussion on procrastination? As the above study suggests, exercise has plenty of payoffs, among them longevity and an improved lifestyle.

Take my own case, for example. I am sixty-two years old. I

weigh a steady 135 pounds, and I am above five and a half feet tall. I have an excellent appetite and enjoy great health. I am able to work with alertness from nine in the morning until six at night, seeing one client after the other all day long without a break, not even for lunch. I usually have a sandwhich sent in. I hardly ever tire throughout the day.

Four or more times a week I get up at seven o'clock in the morning to do some exercise. I warm up with stretching exercises to make sure I don't pull a muscle. Then I do twenty repetitions of bending over to touch my toes followed by thirty deep knee bends. Then I do twenty or thirty sit-ups, and at least forty push-ups (with my feet one or two steps off the floor). I then jog for twenty minutes, after which I take a shower. That whole sequence takes about thirty minutes, *and I hate it.* But something makes me go down to my recreation room and do it faithfully. When I don't do it, I notice my weight increasing, I get sleepy about two o'clock in the afternoon, and I don't have the vigour and breath that I need to play tennis at least once a week.

Every spring I ski for a week in Colorado. In 1983 I felt confident enough to go down the Aspen race course used by the two Olympic skiers, Bill Johnson and Phil Maher, during the World Cup Race of 1983–4. I went down that run not once but about six times.

On a trip to the Caribbean about ten years ago I snorkelled for the first time. One of the most memorable days of that whole trip, and in fact in my whole life, was when I dived for live conch. I was with my wife Marcie and our friends Tom and Sallie Lundeen. We anchored in a small bay and we could see the conch on the ocean floor about twenty-five feet down. Tom dived first and came up with one, triumphantly holding it high. That spurred me on to do the same. I felt my lungs ready to burst as I was about three quarters of the way down but still managed to touch the bottom, grab a shell, and head for the surface. I did that twice that day and never felt prouder in my life. I then realized my exercising and dieting had paid off.

Those were great times because I paid my dues and felt like a winner. I could do something a lot of men my age would never think of doing.

The Aerobic System

There's nothing special about my being able to dive for conch. You could do it, too. Physical fitness is within the reach of anyone, and almost any exercise programme you take up will benefit you, though of course it is important to consult your doctor before you start.

One exercise programme I can recommend is that devised by Dr Kenneth H. Cooper and described in his book *The New Aerobics*. He tells you in detail how much exercise you should do, how often, and how long it should take, taking your age into account. Someone of my age — over fifty — would aim, for example, to walk three miles in 36–43½ minutes five times a week, which is quite a brisk walk! Or run a mile in 6–8½ minutes six times a week, or two miles in 13–16 minutes three times a week. The targets are tabulated by age, and there are tables for other sports like cycling, swimming and squash.

If you start such a programme you will probably find it a real struggle at first, as I did, but that as you become stronger you don't worry about those tables, you simply do more and more exercise until you feel you are getting enough. The more you do (within reason) the better you feel and the more you want to do. But stick to it even if your progress is slow. As I've said before, the slightest progress is still progress.

Vices

Cigarette smoking, alcohol, drugs, and poor diet are the major vices that will rob you of your health and age you prematurely. Two hundred thousand people in the United States died in 1984 from lung and colon-rectal cancer. The likelihood of getting cancer is fifteen times greater for smokers than for non-smokers. And the survival rate of these cancer patients is about 70%. Similar statistics can be pointed to regarding the abuse of alcohol, nicotine, and certain foods. And the pity of it all is that it is not necessary to give up any of these vices *totally* in order to be a healthy person. I drink and I eat wonderful meals, but all in *moderation*. The only vice I avoid is street drugs. I have never tried marijuana or any other street drug. I feel I'm high enough most of the time without the help of these chemicals and I don't want to start other bad habits.

But let me tell you about my smoking and my drinking habits. I started smoking cigarettes and pipes when I was in the army at the age of 18. I didn't like cigarettes and tried inhaling them for a short period of time but wisely gave that up. I did enjoy pipe smoking but didn't inhale the smoke. I liked to concentrate with a pipe in my mouth and the smoke swirling up in front of me. I'm the kind who likes to sit and ponder and it is so much nicer to do that when curled up in a chair with my favourite pipe.

So I learned to smoke pipes for a number of years and then when I finished post-graduate studies I also learned to smoke cigars. I loved cigars and smoked them and pipes all day long. However, about ten years ago I decided to give them both up because I could just see my cheeks or gums develop cancer. So I decided to stop the whole business all together.

Drinking, too, is something I do in moderation. I think I can have my cake and eat it too as long as I do it sensibly. Practically every night of my adult life I will have a glass of wine or a highball after I come home and before dinner. When I go to a restaurant I will almost invariably have a glass or two of wine. And when I am at a friend's home I will certainly enjoy a glass or two of whatever is being offered. This has been going on for thirty years and I have not lost control once in the past thirty years.

Food? I know about good food. I value good food, and I love eating in good restaurants. But I don't overdo it. I don't stuff myself, although those around me know that I have a fine appetite. But if I have had enough to eat I might let the dessert go entirely. I seldom have ice cream or chocolate. If I do, I won't have another treat for a day or two. If I have steak one day, in order to keep my fat and cholesterol levels low, I will make sure I do not have steak normally again for the rest of that week. If I have eggs for breakfast more than twice a week, I will see to it that I have cereal with skimmed milk the other days. I don't use butter or salt on my corn any longer because I have learned to do without them although I enjoy butter and salt on corn. I try not to drink more than three cups of coffee a day and not to drink colas or soda pop. They contain caffeine and sugar.

Mostly I eat fish and chicken, with the skin of the chicken removed. Most of the preparation is done by broiling or baking rather than frying. My salads are less often doused with the creamy dressings such as roquefort, thousand island, or french; instead I use lemon juice, a vinaigrette dressing, or a little wine vinegar, and a little oil. Excess must be balanced with restraint.

Dieting

Ever since Western society has become figure conscious we have been going on one diet after another doing such strange things as drinking eight glasses of water a day or eating nothing but grapefruit. I suppose this was inevitable because we became desperate for some way to keep our weight down once we realized that being heavy was really quite dangerous to our health. Dieting seemed to be the answer. Now, however, increasing evidence is emerging which indicates that dieting often simply doesn't work. In fact, about 95% of the people who lose weight will regain it later. Not only that, they often add to their previous weight.

The body apparently has an inner sense of how much it should weigh. It reaches a 'set point' which is a weight any person will reach and maintain if the normal eating patterns are not disturbed or manipulated. The body fights any attempt to change the weight from this set point, whether it be up or down.

It seems to be determined by physical factors in the body, not those which society sets as standards for health or beauty.

Modern research indicates that when you starve yourself the body becomes more efficient in using what little food you are taking in so that the weight can be maintained. In addition, the body not only uses up the fat, but also the muscle. To reduce the further loss of body mass, the body becomes fatigued so that the person will slow down and not use up more energy.

In time the body becomes accustomed to a certain calorie intake but not for long. People tend to go off their diets, but not completely. They eat less than they use to, but more than they ate when they were fully on a complete diet. This little surplus is enough to cause them to regain weight since the body has learned to do with less. This is actually another form of overeating but it doesn't restore the muscle tissue, it puts back fat. When this happens a number of times, a person has 'more fat mass and less lean mass', according to psychologist Dr Joseph Maciejko. In short, even at the same weight level before the diet, the dieter is now 'fatter than before'.

But, according to Dr Maciejko, who writes in *Renaissance*, an American newsletter on eating disorders, that's not the end of the story. The body will remember going through these diets and apparently becomes less effective in being able to lose weight each time a diet is used thereafter. For example, if a laboratory rat is put on a diet and is allowed to eat normally later, it will regain the weight it lost. But if it is on a diet a second time, it takes twice as long to lose the same amount of weight. After this happens it takes three times as long.

Reports from the University of California at Berkeley offer the same findings: cutting down calories may simply not be enough to change weight. Apparently some people who are prone to obesity will burn up calories at a lower rate than others, even when they are performing the same activity.

Obviously the last word has not been said about weight control and it behoves all of us to keep in touch with the periodic reports in magazines, health letters, books, and lectures on the subject. I subscribe to a couple of health magazines, which are prominently displayed in my offices. I take health newsletters which keep me informed of the latest findings on good eating habits, proper exercise and general health tips. Self-interested people make the effort to find out about these things; they take the time to read or watch programmes on television that have to do with these subjects. They become well informed so they can take control over their lives. How sensible that is.

The information I have given you here, if you were to follow it, even as incomplete as it is, will help you live healthier and longer. And don't forget the greater pleasure you will have from being more active, looking better, and being able to engage in activities which you could not if you were feeble or very heavy.

Wealth

A not infrequent way in which people neglect themselves is that they never make as much of their money as they would if they knew some of the facts of finance. A great deal of money passes through the hands of most people in a lifetime. Some of them can use it well enough to end up with a very nice retirement income while others find themselves broke. And of course there have always been people who enjoy very comfortable incomes all of their lives, who were in the rich bracket, but because they did not care or did not understand anything about money and how to use it or make it grow, frittered it away in a splurge of indulgence over a period of months or years, and wound up with almost nothing in the end.

One of the saddest ways to neglect yourself is simply to be stupid about the handling of money. As I have tried to emphasize several times in this book, money brings enormous comfort, psychological security, health, and power. And I think all of those results are well worth struggling for and planning for. Money is certainly one very respectable and practical way in which to get them.

But as I have also previously indicated, one of the big problems is that money seems to have a bad reputation. People apologize for making the stuff, they feel guilty for making it important in their lives, they are referred to as misers, as tight-fisted, stingy, and just plain disgusting because they put such a high priority on earnings, profits, and savings.

Get rid of these ridiculous notions or you will go down the drain with all those who have these same ideas. Money is simply a convenient way that people show how much they have worked. Not especially so in the case of someone who was given money through an inheritance. But even the inherited money had to be earned by someone who worked very hard or had in some cases just incredible good luck to hit oil, strike a gold vein, or bet on the state lottery and win a few million dollars.

Leaving aside those lucky few who have made their fortunes in these quick ways there still remains the slow but surer way of becoming financially independent if you know some of the basic rules. If you learn them, you will be doing yourself the greatest service and helping your family as well. Then you won't be as a number of my clients have been who, when their factories shut down, had to go look for another job but found that relocating to another state where the employment was better was no easy task. Some of these people had only a car to show for twenty years of making very good wages. Some did not have part ownership in their own homes because they rented. Some did not own antiques, or anything else they could convert into cash because they spent practically everything they earned. When the earnings stopped and the job dried up, they were out on the street in the same shape they were twenty years before with nothing to their names.

That's a financial disaster. And it's practically totally unnecessary. Those people neglected themselves just as surely as if they had taken their money and their belongings and put them outside on the sidewalk of their homes and walked away from them. It was practically ordained they would wind up broke, desperate, and depressed because they had nothing to show for their many years of labour except the fine times they had living from day to day but which, now that they are unemployed, mean nothing. You cannot eat or live from a memory. If you do not put money away for the future you will suffer in the future. This is just a form of procrastination. Boasting that you did it your way or that you had a real ball in the process does not soften the suffering you will have to go through if you do not use your hard work as a way of preparing yourself for the day when you will not be able to work.

Mark Olver Haroldsen, in his book *How to Wake Up The Financial Genius Inside You*, makes the point that half of the population has only a very vague notion of how compounding of money operates. He cites the case of offering people two propositions: the first is to give you the choice of taking $1000 a day for thirty-five days, and the second choice is to take a cent and double it everyday for thirty-five days. Which offer would you consider the best?

Under the first offer you would obviously have $35,000 at the end of the thirty-five days. However, if you take one cent and double it every day for thirty-five days you would have the astounding figure of $171,798,691.80 on the thirty-fifth day.

No matter which financial book I read I always come across this piece of advice: if you want to become financially independent as you get older you must save money, invest it, and let it compound. All the authorities strongly suggest that if you want to get started on your own financial plan, and you happen not to hit an oil well, then start paying yourself 10% of everything you earn as your own nest egg. Don't spend any of it, just simply let it build up.

When you have enough money to invest in a business, real estate, collectibles, stamps, or stocks, etc., do so. Let the money you saved work for you. Think of these dollars as labourers, giants with great power that are able to do something for you even while you're asleep in your bed, or on vacations, or loafing around at weekends. Those dollars are always working if you know how to invest them.

Once you have a nest egg you are cautioned never to spend any of it. Always live on less than you earn. And as you earn more, pay yourself more. It is estimated that only one person out of 100 at retirement age is wealthy, four are financially independent, five are still working at sixty-five, thirty-six will die, and fifty-four will be broke.

Let's see what happened if you did some investing of the type which is common in the mid-1980s. If you took $5000 and invested it at 5% for fifteen years, you would have a total of $10,395. If you invested $5000 at 10% then you would have $20,886 in fifteen years. Notice now, those figures apply to a single lump sum which you invested at one time. But let's see what happens if you were to add a certain amount of money to your investment each year. Now, $5000 at 5% *every* year for fifteen years would yield $133,288. The actual money you would have invested out of your pocket would have been $5000 for fifteen years, or $75,000. You would have earned $38,275 on the money that you invested. And since 5% is really quite low these days let's be more realistic about the percentage of return and use the 10% figure. If you invested $5000 each year at 10% for fifteen years, you would receive a total of $174,749. Here your net return is almost $100,000 and you have more than doubled your money. Now think of doing this not for fifteen years but for thirty years. Time is a crucial factor in getting financial independence. For example, at 10% your money will double every 7.2 years. So if you could guarantee yourself a 10% rate of return, in approximately fifteen years your money would have doubled once and then once again. And if we're talking about investing money for a period of thirty years, your money will double four times. For example, if you could invest $1000 a year for thirty years at 10%, you would at the end of 30 years have $180,943 for your effort. Mind you, that's only $1000 a year. You spend that much on dry cleaning, or perhaps on lawn and garden materials or on electronic equipment, eating out, or vacations. That is the beauty of compounding.

I'm not an economist and there is a great deal about money that I don't know. Therefore I don't want to carry this discussion much beyond this point because I would be out of my element. But I do want to caution you that being bright and educated doesn't mean that you're going to know what to do with money. Those trained to do jobs which pay them enough to make their lives comfortable are not taught *how* to invest money as part of their training. I have had to learn some of these things much later than I should have and I'm sorry I didn't start a more sensible handling of my funds years ago.

Recommendations

Don't adopt the attitude that you want to live today because tomorrow you may die. That's not really quite accurate. The truth of the matter is that you probably won't die for years to come. Insurance companies are willing to insure you for that very reason.

Go to money-management classes that may be given in your local colleges or that may be advertised in newspapers by experts that travel the circuit. These are well worth the few dollars they cost, that is, if they are teaching you about money management. Some of them want to sell you an investment programme or a course in real estate purchasing, and so forth. I can't comment on those since I have never taken one. But I have been to college courses that taught me about stocks, insurance, wills, mutual funds, and banks. Even if the course is an introductory one, all the better. You'll find that you'll learn something of value and it may whet your appetite to attend other classes that are more advanced.

I also recommend that you read books on money management. Or if that's too much for you, at least get a weekly or monthly financial newsletter. I have subscribed to two such letters and have always learned more as a result of this steady exposure.

One of the most important things you can do with some of your money is to buy consultation with a financial adviser. I especially recommend going to one who has nothing to sell except his services. He's not pushing his insurance, his real estates plans, or any such thing. He simply is educating you as to what you might do with your money and it may be the best money you ever spent.

Don't make the assumption that somehow the management of money is common knowledge and that you know as much about it as anyone else does. That simply is not true. It's the same argument I sometimes encounter from people who wonder why they should be visiting a clinical psychologist. They, too, think that they have all the answers about human behaviour, completely ignoring the fact that we spend eight years at college studying the subject. I *do* know a great deal the average person doesn't know about human interaction and psychopathology. I sincerely believe that money spent in seeking my counsel is generally well spent. I take the same attitude about the financial adviser who knows his business or the mechanic who knows his. We all have our specialities and it makes good sense to seek us out when you need something that we know.

8

Hold Your Head High

Thank you for being with me throughout these pages. I hope my writing has been convincing and will urge you on to care better for yourself. This is a task that will require much energy for the rest of your life. There is always a force from society and a force within you that tends to diminish you. These two forces see you as worthless and insignificant. Unless you are aware of their constant presence, you will eventually succumb to their declarations of your inferiority and your worthlessness.

In this book I have tried to show you how you resist these outer and inner voices that tell you you're unworthy. Hold your head high and fill your heart with hope. Do not let the pessimism of the world drown you in messages of despair. You are a member of the human race, the most spectacular achievement in our world. Though you are imperfect, you are far more gifted than you are faulty.

Accept yourself with your shortcomings if you cannot alter them. With guidance and hard work, however, you can reduce your weaknesses and your flaws to a point where they do not interfere with your enjoyment of life.

Stop neglecting yourself. You are not much good to others if you are not good to yourself. When you care for your health, wealth, and your emotions, your critical decisions will either cause you great regret or great joy in years to come, and if you care for who controls your life, you will service yourself and others more efficiently.

Hold your head high, for you are one of a kind. Be proud that even with your limitations you have enough talent, intelligence, and resources to fulfil your destiny to a reasonable degree.

Hold your head high and face the world with curiosity and

gentleness. More often than not others will respond in kind. But if they should not, then do not hesitate to become firm with them, knowing deep in your heart that these are not bad people, they are like you, merely imperfect. But because you value yourself, you will not allow them to abuse you.

However many years you have left on this earth, use them well. Satisfy your deepest desires and needs to a reasonable degree. And always give yourself the attention and the care you would give those you love the most. To show respect for others but not yourself makes a mockery of your best intentions. Teach others the morality of self-acceptance by setting an example of it in yourself.